Whitewash, Red Stone

Whitewash, Red Stone

a history of church architecture in Goa

Paulo Varela Gomes

YODA PRESS

YODA PRESS
268 A/C Vasant Kunj
New Delhi 110070

Published in India
by YODA PRESS

First Published 2011

ISBN 978-93-80403-00-7

Typeset in Bembo Std 11/14.5
By Jojy Philip, New Delhi 110 015
Printed at G.H. Prints, New Delhi 110 020
Published by Arpita Das, YODA PRESS, New Delhi

To my father who told me about Goa when I was a child

To David M. Kowal who welcomed me to Goa when I came here
for the first time and introduced me to the churches of Goa

To Patricia Vieira who encouraged me to write this book and
is responsible for most good things that I have done

Contents

List of Illustrations

Chapter 2

Chapter 3

Chapter 4

Epilogue

Acknowledgements

Very few people contributed to this book. It was solitary work and I am afraid it will show. But the librarian of the Xavier Centre of Historical Research at Alto Porvorim, Goa, Ms Aarti Fernandes, always found any bibliographical references I looked for, no matter how obscure or uncertain. My friend and Goan erudite Percival de Noronha, my friends Rochelle Pinto and Jason K. Fernandes, all took the trouble to read parts of the typescript and make valuable comments. With the Portuguese anthropologist Manuel Magalhães I discussed issues fundamental to this book. Rochelle Pinto, Jason K. Fernandes and Stanley Valladares Smith graciously edited the text. Only those who have ever done editing work – and I have – can fully appreciate the generosity of Rochelle, Jason and Stanley. But, of course, I owe a full-fledged and committed editing job to my editor Arpita Das. When the readers feel that the book is written in decent English they know whom to thank. The editors at Yoda Press, especially Arpita Das, have been enthusiastic and patient – one may say that this is what all editors are, but I know better.

All photographs are by the author unless otherwise indicated.

Introduction I

The Goaness of Goan Churches and Other Problems

The Catholics of Goa and other former Portuguese possessions in India created churches and houses that are unique in the world history of architecture. These buildings appeared in Goa and have been known since the mid-twentieth century as Indo-Portuguese architecture. They represent one of the more remarkable contributions to the history of building from outside European regions where Christian art and architecture matured in the early modern and the modern Ages: Italy, Spain, France, Flanders, Central Europe.

Goa's Indo-Portuguese architecture is different from the Catholic architecture that we see along the coast of the Indian states of Maharashtra and Gujarat (in what was formerly the Portuguese *Província do Norte*, the Northern Province of Portuguese-controlled India), in Kerala, along the Coromandel, or in Bengal. But the common elements in the Catholic architecture of all these regions originated in Goa and these commonalities are far more important than what differentiates its several regional identities. Indo-Portuguese architecture also presents similarities with churches and houses in Brazil, which was Portuguese-dominated in the 16th, 17th and 18th centuries, but it is very different from them, and even more so from the Catholic architecture of Spanish-speaking Latin America or the Philippines.

Catholic architecture in Indian soil originated in the early 16th century as a creation of Portuguese architects, masons and military engineers, and of priests imbued with Portuguese architectural and artistic culture. Later in the same century members of religious orders from several regions of Europe enriched that tradition with their own artistic leanings.

During the 17th century, the first elements of a specifically Indian type of Catholic architecture began to appear in Goa, in the Northern Province, in Kerala, and in some other places. Such was the case of vaulting systems of probable Flemish origin, and of internal elevation types that originated within Jesuit culture and had not previously been built anywhere in the world, to name but two important typological innovations. At the end of the 17th century, these and other elements had coalesced in Goa into a church-type that can be termed the Goan church.

My main purpose in this book is to tell the history of the evolution of church architecture in Goa from the 16th to the 20th centuries in order to answer as simply as possible the following questions: What is a Goan church? When and how did the characteristically Goan church appear? How did it evolve architecturally? How can one explain the fact that an original type of Catholic church appeared in a territory as small as Goa?

In this introduction, I will outline my answer to the last of these questions, that is, I will offer a general explanatory idea about why Goan churches are the way they are and have evolved the way they have. In the subsequent chapters I will try to discuss and substantiate this idea as I trace the chronological history of church building in Goa.

The book begins at the city of Old Goa. Throughout the 16th century, from the Portuguese conquest of 1510 onwards, the City of Goa was the only place where important churches appeared. Unfortunately only one building of those times has survived until the present in

View of Old Goa from the church of N.S. do Monte

its 16th century form: the church of Nossa Senhora do Rosário (Our Lady of the Rosary). Various other significant churches built in the middle decades of the 16th century have subsequently disappeared: the original Cathedral, the Jesuit S. Paulo (St. Paul), the Dominican church, and others. Chapter 1 of this book begins by discussing the church of Our Lady of the Rosary and the few available traces from the other early churches. The second part of the chapter analyzes the parish churches built in the territory known as Ilhas because it is composed of several islands (Tiswadi, Divar, Chorão, Juá) around the City of Goa that were first conquered by the Portuguese.

The churches built in Ilhas were all transformed during the transition between the 16th and the 17th centuries. The same happened to the initial churches built in the other parts of Goa conquered by the Portuguese in the 16th century, Salcete and Bardez (which, together with Ilhas, form the Old Conquests), after parishes were constituted there in 1552. Church building in the 16th century outside of the city of Old Goa was a hasty affair with little artistic concern and only towards the very end of the century did architecturally significant buildings begin to appear.

Chapter 2 of the book deals with the architectural cycle that took place at Old Goa in the transition between the 16th and the 17th centuries and resulted in the substantial transformation of existing churches. Most of the buildings we can see today at the site resulted from profound alteration or redesign of previous churches between 1590 and the 1640s or were built anew during these decades: the Cathedral, the church of the Bom Jesus, the Augustinians, Santa Mónica, Our Lady of the Mount. This cycle of artistic splendour triggered the renovation of churches outside the Old City, throughout Ilhas, Bardez and Salcete.

This cycle was still unfolding when a new architectural flourishing took place in Goa in the mid-17th century and from then on to the early decades of the 1700s. It was during this period that the other still existing famous monuments of Old Goa were built: the Franciscan convent church (Holy Spirit), the church of S. Caetano, the convent premises of Bom Jesus with St. Francis Xavier chapel, the convents of Cruz dos Milagres (Miraculous Cross) and S. João de Deus (St. John of God). Some of these new buildings introduced new architectural themes and types that would be instrumental in the creation of the Goan church. This is the matter I will discuss in Chapter 3.

This spate of construction must have corresponded to a period of economic and social prosperity, but it goes against received knowledge about the historical evolution of Goa, which paints the 17th and 18th centuries as a time of 'decline'. The erection of these buildings therefore, forces us to re-examine the myths of current history that suggest the idea that the City of Goa had no other history but that of downfall and decline in the 17th century.

Decline did indeed become manifest, but a while later, at the beginning of the 18th century, as if suddenly. A symbol of this turning point is the publication of the famous *Edital* of 1719 by Viceroy Ericeira, a law enforcing proclamation: 'I have been informed of the deformity that has befallen this City on account of so many Noble Houses that have been ruined in the last few years in such a manner that inner streets and even major thoroughfares are devoid of inhabitants...' This happens, claims the Viceroy, because the inhabitants of Old Goa make use of the 'devious industry *(a cavilosa industria)* of dismantling the roofs of their houses so that Winter as it enters the walls brings them down...' (winter referring obviously to the rainy season of the south-west monsoon). They do so, the Viceroy continues, to build houses in the villages around the old capital, a proceeding that he prohibits commanding his subjects to restore their houses in Old Goa.

It was useless. The destruction of the Old City had begun, and inaugurated one of the more extraordinary enterprises of urban un-doing in the history of the world, when a city that was once one of the great metropolises of Asia was deliberately dismantled by its inhabitants stone by stone, over the course of two centuries, the 18th and the 19th, until nothing remained of it but the handful of churches that we see today.

It so happens that the destruction of Old Goa corresponded chronologically, culturally and socially to the construction of Goan architecture, especially Goan church architecture. In the course of Chapter 3, I will discuss facts that seem to demonstrate that the Goan church-type appeared at the end of the second cycle of architectural prosperity that occurred in the city of Old Goa in the second half of the 17th century and as a direct consequence of this cycle.

The architecture of Goan churches after the 16th century is far less Portuguese-influenced than one would be led to believe. Goan Catholic architecture certainly is a current originated in Europe, there can be no doubt about it. But apart from its European origin, the European inputs that influenced Goan builders and patrons from the 16th to the 20th centuries did not originate from Portugal alone and sometimes did not originate from Portugal at all. Certain essential typological traits in Goan churches simply do not exist in Portuguese architecture. They bring to our memory places like northern and central Italy (exterior side elevations, niches along the interior of the naves), or Flanders (vaulting systems). This is hardly surprising considering that the religious orders within which most architects of Goan churches were trained in the 16th and 17th centuries were multi-national bodies with priests of pan-European origin or who had travelled extensively throughout Europe. It is also true that Goan church architecture maintained a Portuguese appearance across five centuries. This is due to the habit of whitewashing the exterior and interior of buildings that is characteristic of some southern European regions, such as southern Portugal, and also owed to the fact that, like most Portuguese churches, the churches of Goa are 'poor', at least in Western classical architecture terms: there is little ornamental sculpture in stone; no marble or other valuable stone facing; limited rich stone carving of architectural mouldings. This material austerity is 'compensated' by the use of stucco ornament over vaults and profiles, softly moulded decorative architectural sculpture, the installation of wooden and gilded altars and pulpits. These features are typically Iberian, not Italian or French.

After telling the story of the crucial years which marked the transition between the 17th and the 18th centuries, Chapter 4 will concentrate on the full development of Goan church architecture in the 18th century when local communities (*comunidades*) or powerful local hierarchs (*gaunkars*) took over the reconstruction of the churches founded by the Jesuits or the Franciscans and transformed them into buildings of a new type. The whole of Goa (Ilhas, Bardez and Salcete) was covered by a 'white mantle of churches', to use a phrase coined in 11th-century Europe to signify an epoch of extensive religious and architectural renewal. Some of these new churches were radically different from previous ones and constitute the first Goan churches worthy of this designation.

The case for architectural difference has already been made for the so-called Goan House. Scholars (Carita 1995; Silveira 2008), tourism operators and citizens in general, both in Goa

Catholic house in Goa, 18th–19th century

and internationally, have agreed that the houses built in Goa by upper- and middle-class Catholic landowners essentially in the 18th, 19th and early 20th centuries constitute an extraordinarily coherent and distinct current in the panorama of housing around the world. These houses are now being named 'Portuguese Houses' perhaps because of the influence of tourism since 'Portuguese' is a more exotic denomination than Goan for Indian, British, Russian and other tourists. There is no need to point out that houses such as those of Goa exist nowhere in any town or village in Portugal, Brazil or Portuguese-influenced Africa. They are solely Goan.

The architectural and artistic distinction, in houses as well as churches, has generally been explained with the concepts of 'encounter' between East and West, 'fusion' or 'influence'. I would even say it has been explained away, given the simplicity of the concepts and the nonchalance with which they are used. According to these narratives, Goan churches – and Indo-Portuguese art at large – display a 'mixture' or a 'blend' of Western and Oriental 'motives' or 'traits', the dose of which varies according to time, place and circumstance, almost like a recipe for a dish, the end result being original and somewhat exotic, but always something which is 'this and that', a sum, a combination, a hybrid.

The reason for the hybrid character of Goan church architecture has often been explained as a result of the fact (more often than not undocumented by building documents) that they would have been ornamented by converted local craftsmen and artists, and also, sometimes, by Hindu or Muslim painters, artisans and sculptors, in defiance of the Church Provincial Council's prohibitions issued in the 16th and the 17th centuries.

To me, this explanation, as all others based on 'influences' and 'contacts', fails to account for the character and integrity of the churches of Goa. It is true that, analysing the buildings in parts, this entablature here, this door frame there, this tower, this vault, one can see Portuguese wall composition, Flemish vaulting or ornament, Bijapuri tower design, Konkan stucco patterns and ornamental design, etc. But the churches as overall buildings did not result from the sum of their constitutive parts. Their builders and patrons knew how they wanted a Catholic church to look and how they wanted it to be experienced. Their understanding, I believe, was not Portuguese, Flemish or Indian but Goan Catholic or Indo-Portuguese, if you like. To anyone with architectural and artistic sensitivity, these churches don't seem to be the end-result of a compromise but the affirmative artistic statement of a cultural position.

It is my contention that Indo-Portuguese architecture and art developed its characteristics because it became the more important manifestation of the material culture of a group of people which came into being in the 16th and 17th centuries as a result of conversion to Catholicism – a group of people who had to create a distinct culture for themselves.

In this context, the churches of Goa in the second half of the 17th century and later, were not buildings imposed upon Goans, or buildings negotiated between Goans and foreign prelates or authorities. As we shall see in the course of this book, they were buildings by Goans, designed by Goan architects and masons, including Goan Catholic priests, and, in many cases, commissioned by Goan landowners or Goan local communities. Indeed the first two fully Goan churches were, in my view, Santana (Saint Anne) at Talaulim, begun in 1682, and Nossa Senhora da Piedade (Our Lady of Mercy) at Divar, begun in 1699. It is very likely that they were both designed by Goan priests, Francisco do Rego (1638-1689) and António João de Frias (1664-1727), respectively. One could put it this way: Goan churches were 'native' buildings. The expression 'native clergy' was used in the 19th century to describe the protagonists of a polemic that took place within the Catholic Church from the 16th to the 18th centuries around the accession to the sacred orders of people from India. In close articulation with this polemic, another issue tore Indian Catholicism apart: the conflict between the Portuguese *Padroado Régio* (the right of the Portuguese monarchs to appoint bishops to India and other overseas territories) and the Roman *Propaganda Fide* (the papal agency created at the beginning of the 17th century to take care of matters of overseas

Church of N.S. da Piedade, Divar, frontal façade, early 18th century

evangelization). The two issues converged in the final years of the 17th and the early 18th centuries, precisely the time of the birth of Goan Catholic architecture.

We don't know much about the issue of the native clergy (Melo: 1955; Boxer: 1961 and 1970; Rocha: 1973, 176 ff; 1992 and 1999; Lopes: 1999, 135ff). What we do know can be summarized in the following paragraphs.

Until the suppression of the Jesuits by the Marquis of Pombal, prime minister of King D. José of Portugal, in the mid-18th century, there was 'no real seminary in the Tridentine sense' to train priests in Portuguese India despite numerous decisions by the provincial councils in Goa to establish a seminary to form Indians for the priesthood, from the mid-16th century onwards (Melo: 1955: 143). There was of course the College of Santa Fé (Holy Faith), established in 1541 and given by the Crown to the Jesuits. The Dominicans had the College of St. Thomas (1596), the Franciscans the College of St. Bonaventure (1602), the Augustinians the College of Our Lady of Pópulo (1602). But the effectiveness of these establishments in the formation of an influential Goan clergy was minimal (Melo: 1955: 164 ff).

There were however some active priests of Goan origin since the mid-16th century, a fact that proved to be instrumental in the origin of Goan Catholic architecture. In a report submitted to the *Propaganda Fide* in Rome after 1655, the Portuguese priest Pedro Borges, who had been in Goa as Secretary to the Inquisition, gives the figures of the distribution of parishes in Goa by regular and secular priests, European and native Goan (Melo: 1955: 156 ff). According to this report the disproportion between the situation in Ilhas and in the rest of Goa was startling: the European priests of the regular orders (essentially Jesuits in Salcete, Franciscans in Bardez, Dominicans and Augustinians in Ilhas) took care of practically all the parishes in Bardez and Salcete, 23 and 25 respectively. In the Old City, all the existing 11 parishes were in the hands of European regular priests. In Ilhas, however, there were 21 parishes manned by secular Goan priests. Europeans were in charge of only 5 parishes.

This rather startling fact is confirmed by other sources and documents, beginning with the Jesuit chronicle by Sebastião Gonçalves, written circa 1614: almost all the parishes in Ilhas were *a conta dos Clerigos naturaes desta terra* (in the hands of clerics hailing from this land) with the exception of Taleigão, Santa Cruz (Holy Cross), Santa Bárbara (St. Barbara) at Morombim-o-Grande and Santa Maria Madalena (St. Mary Magdalen) at Siridão, which were Dominican parishes (Bragança Pereira: 1945: 7). This means that, in Catholic terms, at the beginning of the 17th century, the islands of Tiswadi, Divar, Juá and Chorão, were religiously controlled by Goans.

A likely reason for this to have happened is the action of Archbishop D. frei Aleixo de Menezes (in Goa 1595–1609). He was the first to replace regular priests by native priests in the parishes and to create parishes for Goan priests. He did so precisely in Ilhas where his own order, the Augustinians, was in charge of several parishes (Melo: 1955: 146).

This is probably why 'Goan church architecture' appeared in Ilhas. Talaulim and Divar are villages in Ilhas and, as we shall see in the course of Chapters 4 and 5 of this book, most decisive Goan innovations in church design originated in Ilhas buildings.

In the 1650s, the priests of the Italian Theatine Order (the designation comes from its founder S. Caetano of Thiene) who had arrived in Goa shortly before 1640, began their church in Old Goa, a building that I discuss in Chapter 3. It introduced some architectural novelties in Goa the importance of which should, I believe, be valued bearing in mind that the Theatines were key players in the drama unfolding around the issue of the native clergy and also in view of the growing presence of the *Propaganda Fide* in India to which the Theatines themselves were no strangers (Klaiber 1993). The Theatines in Goa were preaching in favour of giving access to Indians to the Holy Communion at the same time as Goan priests were acting in Goa, Lisbon, and Rome for the right of their brethren to ascend in the hierarchy of the Catholic Church in Portuguese India.

Two priests particularly merit further research: the Goan Mateus de Castro (who was a Brahmin from Divar), and the Portuguese Pedro Borges. There were certainly others. There are historiographical publications which mention memorials sent to the King of Portugal and to the Pope by Goan Brahmins in the first half of the 17th century (Melo 1955: 154). Mateus de Castro (Melo 1955: 215 ff) arrived in Rome in 1625, was ordained in 1630, and came back to Goa in 1633 as *Protonotario Apostolico* in Goa, that is, as an envoy from the Holy See. He returned to Rome later, at an uncertain date to fight for the cause of the native clergy and thus transferred his allegiance to the papal agency, the *Propaganda Fide*. In 1653 he wrote in defence of the Brahmin clergy, *Espelho dos Bracmanes* (The Mirror of Brahmins).

Even the sketchy data published so far about Mateus de Castro, Pedro Borges and other Goan priests (also see Xavier 2008: 417 ff) make it abundantly clear that the Goan clergy affair was used by several anti-Portuguese powers and institutions: *Propaganda Fide*, to begin with, but also, to a large extent, France and the French cardinals in Rome. France was at war with the Iberian powers and, in the papal capital, the French tried to promote their candidates to the papal throne against Spanish or Spanish-favoured Cardinals and to place their own missionaries in the Middle East and Asia. Another enemy of the Portuguese was the Papacy itself, which, one should not forget, did not recognize the new Portuguese dynasty, that of the Braganças, which had assumed power after a coup in 1640 against the Spanish kings who had ruled Portugal since 1580 and who were Rome's number one ally in Europe. Then, there was the Dutch East India Company that tried to take advantage of Mateus de

Castro's conspiracy to evict the Portuguese from Goa (Ahmad 2008). And last – but by no means the least – the more important political, military and cultural power in mid-17th century Deccan: the Sultanate of Bijapur. In 1654, Mateus de Castro was in Bijapur and he seems to have tried to conspire with the Bijapuri and the Dutch to attack Goa (Kamat 1987), although this story needs some qualification and clarifying (Ahmad 2008: 322ff).

Bijapur can only be termed a Muslim power in the over-simplifying language and ideologies of colonial historiography and of contemporary partisan sloganeering. It was to a large extent, like the other Deccanese monarchies or the Mughal Sultanate, a power seeking to maintain a balance among its different subjects, including Christians and the many foreigners seeking employment in the court. Several Catholic priests travelled to Bijapur and Golconda. *Propaganda Fide* missions were established in Deccan kingdoms. It is therefore only natural that Christian envoys (and spies, including those of the Portuguese Viceroy) swarmed the court of Bijapur. Taking advantage of a rebellion in Bardez in 1654, a Bijapuri commander, probably instigated by Mateus de Castro, invaded the region (Ibid.: 323–24). The plot, half-heartedly prepared, failed; Mateus de Castro fled to Rome in 1656, and died there in 1677.

Fr. Pedro Borges, like Mateus de Castro before him, transferred his allegiance to the *Propaganda* via the intermediation of the Bijapuris who helped him reach Rome where granted audience by the Pope twice in 1656 (Melo 1955: 156 ff), he did devastating harm to the Portuguese *Padroado* with his writings. Rome, France, the Dutch, and Bijapur, all used the issue of the Goan priests to try and undermine Portuguese power in India. But, of course, Goan priests also tried to take advantage of these events to favour their cause and to put pressure on the Portuguese crown and on the Church using the threat of reverting to anti-Portuguese forces. This, after all, was politics.

In 1658 Rome issued the Constitution *Sacrosancti Apostolatus Officii* to the Vicar Capitular of Goa in which the regular and secular European clergy in Goa were accused of replacing native priests without need and denying them access to parishes even when the European priests did not speak Indian languages. A decree by the *Propaganda Fide* of the same year tried to redress these wrongs (Melo 1955: 150 ff). In 1677 and 1678 Archbishop D. António Brandão allowed himself to be involved in a violent conflict with the Jesuits of Salcete about his right of visitation to their parishes, vehemently denied by them. D. António excommunicated the Jesuits and threatened to hand over the churches of Salcete to the 'native clerics' (Melo 1955: 178), another instance of the Goan clergy's cause being at the same time the cause of a conflict and a weapon used in other conflicts, in this case the one between the Archbishop and the religious orders.

The same happened again at the beginning of the 18th century in Bardez when Archbishop

Ignacio de Santa Theresa (1721–39) tried to replace the Franciscans with native priests at the head of parishes and provoked a full-fledged rebellion among the clergy (Nazaré 1897: 237 ff). Archbishop Santa Theresa engaged in successive conflicts with the Viceroy and the religious orders, especially the Jesuits and the Augustinians, his own congregation, around several issues, the more important of which was his blatant favouring of the Goan clergy (Rocha 1992). In 1682, the first native regular congregation was created in Goa: the Recolhimento de Santa Cruz dos Milagres (Miraculous Cross), formed by three secular native priests from Margão and later joined by Fr. José Vaz who gave them the rule of the Lisbon Oratorians in 1685 (Melo 1955: 176).

Some years later, Goan upper caste clergymen of Brahmin or Chardó origin, were debating in manuscript or print their respective caste merits in public affirmation of a relative triumph of the native clergy in Goan Catholic circles. Two of the more important participants in this debate were none other than the priest-architects of Santana de Talaulim and Piedade de Divar, Francisco do Rego and António João de Frias. This is a very significant fact indeed. The prominent role played by the priests in the literary and ideological arena is inseparable from the highly original form of the buildings that they designed and helps in establishing the cultural complexity of the conjuncture in which Goan church architecture was born.

Goan priests were in charge of Santana de Talaulim since the late years of the 16th century (Mascarenhas 2009). This fact needs clarification because the church had been built as a Jesuit foundation a couple of decades before and it was only made a parish after 1695. In any case, Goan vicars made it a monument to themselves and their Brahmin ancestry: in the pavement of the church we can still see three graves of priests from Goa with inscriptions in Portuguese stating that they were Brahmin (*bracmane*), among which the grave of Francisco do Rego occupies a prominent place before the main altar.

Buildings such as the churches of Santana de Talaulim and Piedade de Divar represent the cultural affirmation of upper caste Goan Catholic priests, probably the first historical testimonies of the independent culture of the Goan Catholic elite. Goan churches as a particular type of Catholic buildings attained full maturity precisely when Goan Catholics began to control their cultural destiny.

The text by Francisco do Rego, *Tratado Apologético contra varias Calumnias impostas pela malevolência contra a sua nação bracmana*, (Apologetic Treaty against the Calumnies proffered by malevolence against his Brahmin Nation), which remained unpublished, and the book by the priest António João de Frias, *Aureola dos Indios & Nobiliaria Bracmane*, (Eulogy of Indians and Brahmin Nobility), published in 1702, are variations of the *Espelho dos Bracmanes* by Mateus de Castro of decades before (1653). Castro, let us recall, was a Divari and a Brahmin, and he is praised as such by Frias in his book.

Fifty years after Castro had conspired with Bijapur to overthrow the Portuguese rule in Goa, a book praising him was written in Goa and then went through all the stages of censorship (Inquisition, Court) to finally be published in Lisbon. This could happen because most of these Goan priests had been to Portugal, had frequented the University at Coimbra and the literary Academies of Lisbon's aristocratic milieu, as proven by the fact that their writings, including the comedies and poems said to have been written by Francisco do Rego, are mentioned by Barbosa Machado's famous *Biblioteca Lusitana* (1741–58) which is among other things a bibliography of academic literature of the late 17th and early 18th centuries. The publication and success of Goan literature was also possible because religious and political things were not perceived as we tend to perceive them now, in modern nationalistic terms. Castro was praised by António João de Frias for his caste, that is, his nobility, and for the fact that he was a Catholic Bishop, regardless of his affiliation with the *Propaganda Fide* or even Bijapur. Frias' book drew a printed response by a Chardó priest, Leonardo Paes: *Promptuario das diffinições indicas* (Glossary of Indian Definitions), published in Lisbon in 1713, a long historical treatise against the Brahmins, in favour of princes and warriors from all over India (including Shivaji!) and of the *gaunkars* of Chardó Salcete villages such as Orlim, Azossim and Carmoná.

One wonders how important caste issues were for the rivalry between parishes and therefore for the choice of the architectural and ornamental solutions of their churches. The articulation of upper caste positions (Brahmin or Chardó) within the Catholic Church of Goa, and therefore within Goan society, is as yet an un-researched story. It is however of the utmost importance for the full understanding of the meaning of Goan church architecture. In fact, Goan Catholics were not a uniform 'community'. They were divided along social, regional, political and linguistic lines and these changed over time. The material culture of Catholics as a whole presents a great deal of coherence, especially vis-à-vis other religious groups, but there are perhaps distinctions between, for instance, a Catholic Brahmin Salcete house and other Catholic houses and between different types of architectural ornament, but in order to establish these distinctions we would need to know far more than we do about who exactly commissioned the more significant churches. In this book I will have to limit myself to treating churches in general terms as Catholic buildings without going into subtler details.

The last chapter of the book deals with the 19th and early 20th centuries, when modern architecture made its appearance in Goa, as it did throughout India, in the form of British inspired neo-gothic. This was but a moment in the history of Catholic architecture in Goa, very few churches having been built in that period. However, it was an intense moment as the Goan-ness of Goan churches was made to coexist, not necessarily in a peaceful manner, with architectural modernity. This is best seen at the more important building that I will discuss in Chapter 5, the remarkable church of Saligão, built after 1867.

Modernity took a very peculiar shape in Goa's churches during the 19th and early 20th centuries: its main characteristic, at least in architectural terms, is that it was not modern at all. I believe this was due to the specific culture of Goan Catholics but also the specific political and religious circumstances of Goan and Indian church life in the 19th century when the conflict between the *Padroado* and *Propaganda* reached its climax. This will be my main argument in the last chapter of the book.

The fact that a distinct Goan church architecture attained full maturity in the second half of the 17th century was first realized by José Pereira in his *Baroque Goa* of 1995 and especially in *Churches of Goa* of 2002, books in which he managed to shake off the vision of things inherited from the pioneering works by the Portuguese historians Mario Tavares Chicó and Carlos de Azevedo, the first to have conducted art history research on Goa in modern terms (1951 to 1969). According to Chicó and Azevedo, after the 'golden' days

Church of N.S. Mãe de Deus, Saligão, Goa, mid-19th century

of the early 17th century's monuments of Old Goa, only the church of the Theatines, S. Caetano (1650s), interrupted the inexorable trend towards decadence (and Baroque, which to them was the same).

Without sharing Chicó and Azevedo's vision of things, David Kowal, the North-American author of a couple of papers that constitute a truly scholarly approach to the history of Goan architecture (1993, 2001), somehow subscribed to their periodization by paying little attention to anything built after 1660, although noting a definite 'indianization' of architectural characteristics from those dates onwards. As Kowal was the first to point out, this was partially due to the Deccan's influences upon Goa's church architecture.

José Pereira gave his idea of a specifically Indian Catholic architecture names and locations: he spoke of an 'Indian Style', and listed five churches he considered of high architectural quality and distinct from whatever had been built before, his 'Indian Baroque Quintet': the Franciscan's Espírito Santo (Holy Spirit) in Old Goa, the Jesuit churches at Margão and Talaulim, and the parish churches of Divar and Juá. This list was perhaps composed because José Pereira likes Quintets: the church at Juá is from the second half of the 18th century and doesn't really belong in the same group as the others. But no matter. To my view, his instinct was right: somewhere between the Franciscan's church and the church at Divar, that is, during the second half of the 17th century, a church type of design the Christian world had never seen before appeared in Goa.

More recently (2005), José Lourenço, a lecturer of Christian art at the Seminary of Rachol authored *The Parish Churches of Goa, a Study of Façade Architecture*. The book contains good frontal photographs (by Pantaleão Fernandes) of every parish church in Goa. Without it my work in this book would have been much more difficult and Lourenço's systematic inventory represents a great service rendered to architectural history and Goan heritage.

Apart from David Kowal's excellent articles however, modern historiography of the architecture of the city of Old Goa comes from Portugal. This historiography however, emerged after, and even as a result of a long hiatus. The fall of Goa, Damão and Diu in 1961 caused a 30-year interruption in the Portuguese scholarly interest in things Goan in the field of architectural history that was ended only in the mid-1990s by a paper published by an architect, José Manuel Fernandes (1994). At more or less the same time, Rafael Moreira, an art historian from the Universidade Nova de Lisboa, published a series of very perceptive articles about the Arch of the Viceroys (1994), the early buildings of Old Goa (1995) and the Theatine church (1997), based on his wide-ranging knowledge of Portuguese and European history.

Pedro Dias, an art historian from the University of Coimbra, has written extensively about the art and architecture of Old Goa (1999). In particular, we owe him decisive studies about the Bom Jesus (1999) and the Cathedral (2003) that were recently included in a monographic essay on the *Velha Cidade* and Panjim (2005).

Vítor Serrão, an art historian from the University of Lisboa, has just published (2008) an article about the architects and artists who worked for the Augustinians at the end of the 16th century, which is the major contribution to date about the architect Júlio Simão and sheds new light on the artistic activity of Goa in his times. The article is based on the author's research at the Goa Historical Archives in Panjim and it demonstrates the plethora of unexplored material at that institution waiting for researchers with a good command of the Portuguese language.

My colleague Walter Rossa at the Department of Architecture of the University of Coimbra, who is Portugal's leading historian of urbanism, has published a decisive essay on Old Goa's urban evolution in the form of a chapter of his book about Indo-Portuguese cities (1997).

The best architectural history book ever written on Old Goa, however, is by António Nunes Pereira: *A Arquitectura Religiosa Cristã de Velha Goa* (Christian Religious Architecture in Old Goa), published in Lisbon in 2005. It was initially written in German and presented as a PhD thesis at the University of Reinisch-Westfallisch in 2003. The book contains the first correct architectural surveys of Old Goa's churches as well as the first professional discussion of their architectural history. It is and will remain invaluable for a long time to come and it is indeed a great shame that the book is not translated into English. Nunes Pereira has also written a very good article on the early history of Old Goa's Cathedral, which is under publication as I write these lines.

As this book demonstrates, facts, hard historical facts about Goan churches, are only established in the case of the city of *Velha Goa*: dates and characteristics of building phases, names of patrons, builders and designers. But even in the case of this city there are more lacunae than certainties in spite of almost two centuries of scholarship initiated by Cotineau de Kloguen's *Historical Sketch of Goa* published under the aegis of the British in 1831.

The disappearance of the city of Goa, of its streets, squares, *terreiros* (large open spaces in front of churches, palaces or noble houses, the North Indian equivalent of which would be *maidan*), *largos* (little squares), *calçadas* (mounting streets), houses and palaces, of most of its churches, chapels and convents, has ensured that every history of the architecture of Goa is necessarily flawed from the beginning. What was built in the *Velha Cidade* by the Viceroy, the religious orders, the Archbishop, the *Senado da Câmara* (Town Hall) and other town and State institutions, and the aristocracy, was the model for the architectural form and type, for the furniture and for the ornament of churches, convents, palaces and houses built throughout Bardez, Salcete and Ilhas. This model has, to a great extent, disappeared without leaving a trace, which means that whatever one writes about the churches of Goa is subject to a disquieting doubt: where does this come from: this moulding, this frame, this vaulting system, this type of façade, these doorway columns? Are we sure they didn't exist somewhere in Old Goa?

We have no precise descriptions and few images of the *Velha Cidade*. Some important churches still stand, the most important of all, the Cathedral, as well as one palatial house (the Archbishop's), a couple of convents (Santa Mónica, the *Casa Professa* – Professed House - of the Bom Jesus, St. John of God). There are 19th-century drawings and early 20th-century photographs of parts of churches. But a lot has vanished with buildings as important for Goan art as the palaces of the Viceroy, the *Senado* and the Inquisition, the churches and convents of the Augustinians, Dominicans, Carmelites. Also gone are the Jesuit, Franciscan, Augustinian and Dominican colleges and the wealthy parish churches of N.S. da Serra and N.S. da Luz (Our Lady of the Hills and Our Lady of Light), among many others. Sacristies and cloisters, altars, pulpits, stuccoes and paintings, vault decorations, have all disappeared.

Scattered through Goa one finds altars, pulpits, images, baptismal fonts, rescued from the *Velha Cidade* while it was systematically dismantled by Portuguese and Goan authorities, and by Goan gentry in the 19th century. The inventory of these 'exiled' works of art was done by careful and caring people. But seeing the altars and pulpits of the Franciscan church of Madre de Deus (Mother of Goa), Daugim at the nave of S. Jerónimo (St. Jerome), Mapuça, where we know that they now stand, is little consolation for the complete and radical disappearance of one of the most celebrated and wealthiest churches of Goa.

At the site of Madre de Deus, among coconut trees and marshes, we can now contemplate with dismay a devastatingly ugly factory spreading rust and garbage around it, and some old stones, barely visible under grime and green. The beautiful landscape celebrated by the writers who mourned the demise of Madre de Deus is still there. But the architecture is gone and with it, the possibility of a serious historical understanding of the past.

As for the rest, as for the hundreds of churches and chapels outside the *Velha Cidade* which constitute the bulk of Goan ecclesiastical architecture, and to me undoubtedly its more Goan and therefore interesting buildings, much was done as far as dates and names are concerned by Filipe Neri Xavier, Bragança Pereira, Ricardo Teles, and particularly by father Gomes Catão in dozens of articles published in Goan journals and newspapers from the 1920s to the 1970s. The results are summarized in Gomes Catão's *Anuário* of the Archdiocese of Goa and Daman (1953 edition), the 'holy book' of church dates for Goa, the source of practically every single subsequent writer.

The data here published was collected from 16th- and 17th-century published chronicles and from other dispersed sources published in the late 19th century by researchers of Goan and European Portuguese origin. In many cases the dates given are not the dates of the church façades, towers, sacristies, lateral galleries and lateral chapels, that we see today. They are building foundation dates, perhaps the dates of the church's perimeter walls. The buildings as they stand are not precisely dated. Words like *reconstruída*, *reedificada* or *reparada* (rebuilt, re-edified, repaired) abound. They mean very little, practically nothing, in architectural terms: to what extent, exactly, was the said church modified, or even rebuilt? Of this we are not informed. However, Father Catão's book is invaluable. All dates that I quote in the present work are from his 1955 *Anuário* unless expressly indicated.

In order to trace the evolution of construction from the the 16th to the 20th centuries one needs to look at the relevant buildings and, by comparing forms, establish the chronological order according to which Goan patrons and architects commissioned and built architectural and decorative elements: to establish a history of forms is the only way to understand the building's evolution. I have attempted to do this but it was not easy and the results are far from satisfactory, especially because some forms never go away and others keep recurring at intervals which are difficult to ascertain or explain: some decorative mouldings over doors and windows that appear for the first time in the mid-18th century, for instance, are still used, without any easily perceptible change, a century and a half later.

In order to be precise at dating and therefore at describing evolution, we would need to have access to a particular kind of written sources – church or administrative records containing building documents. Documents of this type, referring to a handful of churches, have already been used. But even if these sources were to exist in plentiful, they are yet to be located and put to any use. This means that we actually know very little about the chronological evolution of church building in Goa. In the absence of reliable data, some of the chronological ideas in this book are speculative. For example, when I propose that the first false dome, a very interesting Goan 'invention' in church façade design, could have appeared in the building of Santo Estevão (St. Stephen), Juá around 1759, I base this assumption entirely upon the importance of this particular church vis-à-vis others with similar façades – which I think were built much later, over a century later in most cases – and also upon the relevance that the Goan *taluka* of Ilhas had for the development of an autonomous Goan architectural tradition. This suggestion, like some other assumptions of mine, must of course await future research to be proved right.

Introduction II

Church and Landscape

The location of churches in their surrounding territory is one of the more remarkable aspects of Goan religious architecture. Goan churches are landscape monuments. They are not comprehensible without the territory in which they were built; they are not aesthetically enjoyable without their natural setting. One could go as far as to say that they are the most beautiful built ornament of Goa's landscape.

Church of N.S. da Piedade, Divar, seen from the Mandovi river

In spite of the brutal and careless modern development that took place in most of Salcete, Bardez and Ilhas since the 1980s and virtually destroyed vast extensions of these territories, one can still perceive the extraordinary landscape sensitivity that presided over the choice of place and orientation of church builders of the old days.

One of the first things that comes to a European observer's attention is the fact that, contrary to what happens in Europe, churches do not appear to have been built within villages but outside them. This is so surprising that I kept asking myself and bothering friends and colleagues with questions such as: why are Goan churches located at the periphery of villages, having the houses either to their back or to one of their flanks and not before them? Why aren't the churches to be found presiding over squares, dominating the town or village's skyline, or appearing at the end of streets, like in Europe?

I came up with a couple of answers to these questions and so have those with whom I discussed the issue. But none was very good and it was only after some time that I realized that I was asking the wrong questions. Churches do not appear within villages because they were not built within anything that could be called a village in European terms. And this is because there was nothing in Goa resembling the European concept of village, street or square, when the initial churches were built in the 16th and 17th centuries. Furthermore, in the Goan countryside, there still isn't.

There were in Goa in the 16th and 17th centuries, as there are today, cultivated fields and inhabited settlements. Fields and groups of houses were and still are divided along property, family and caste lines and limits. Some circumscriptions of land the inhabitants of Goa named *gaon*, a word the Portuguese authors of the first *forais* (plural for *foral*, the official document establishing rights in a given land) translated as *aldeia* (village). Why they used this particular word to interpret the concept of *gaon* is an interesting question but it need not interest us here. The fact is that these 'villages' did not correspond to their European-Mediterranean image: they had no main or secondary squares with religious buildings or noble dwellings presiding over them; there were no streets and no aligned houses along streetfronts. On the contrary, Portuguese and other European observers were in agreement about describing the settlements along the Konkan and Malabar coasts as devoid of urban form in European terms. The French Pyrard de Laval, who visited Malabar between 1601 and 1610, said of Calicut that 'the houses are not laid out in order, nor aligned along streets like in Europe, but dispersed here and there', and this is an example among many (V. Gomes, 2004). I had discussed these texts from the point of view of what they revealed about the people who wrote them, but the strangeness of the reality they perceived had escaped me.

The extraordinary thing is that the territory of Goa has not changed that much in 500 years: the inhabited landscape of Goa's valleys and plains is still characterized by a kind of continuous stream of human dwellings: houses meander sheltered by the coconut groves as these follow the capricious curves of the open fields (paddy or otherwise) or the coastline. Here and there, one finds religious landmarks: temples, churches, crosses, roadside shrines. The modern state traced the borders of *waddos* (wards), administratively interrupting these flows of human presence. A combination of a certain number of *waddos* was called a village (*aldeia*). Villages sometimes extend for several kilometres along the edges of the open fields so that often there is no real separation between contiguous villages.

Little towns like Panjim, Margão and Mapuça, exist along with other smaller *taluka* centres. These were endowed with signs of urbanity in recent times, the late 18th, the 19th and the 20th centuries: formalized squares, straight streets and roads, town halls and courthouses. Villages however have no centre except the odd (and very recent) Hall or Shopping Mall. They have no squares. And, as they have no centre or squares, they cannot have the church presiding over the central square.

Therefore, how did the Catholic priest or friar who arrived in a non-village territory like Goa in the 16th or 17th centuries choose the location for his church when, to his eyes, human dwellings were everywhere? During long and fruitful discussions with the Portuguese anthropologist Manuel Magalhães who has been studying some Goan villages for years, we both came to realize that the first priests could not have chosen this location at random. European priests must have realized that the inhabited landscape in Goa was not disorganized, contrary to the first, and erroneous, perceptions of more casual observers and travellers. With time, priests understood that dwellings were grouped by caste and profession and that to each group of dwellings corresponded a few landmarks: wells, springs, ponds, shrines and sometimes temples. They also must have understood that the more important social or religious groups sometimes built and controlled larger temples.

It goes without saying that Catholic settlements did not exist at the time, as there were no Catholics. Only after conversion did the Catholic houses start to appear. These new settlements were known by the designation *povoação* and were the first *aldeias* recognizable in European terms. Throughout Goa, but also in the region of Bombay and Daman in the *Província do Norte*, and undoubtedly in many other parts of India, *povoação* is the name still given to Catholic neighbourhoods.

Faced with the existence of several caste or professional circumscriptions, Catholic priests obviously did the sensible thing: they chose for the location of their churches places that could not be identified with any of the existing social or professional groups in particular. At the same time, this allowed them to seek sites that could be seen from afar leaving an impressive mark upon the landscape.

View of the church of Aldona from the south

The Catholic settlements were not built around or in front of the church because the site chosen to locate the church was almost always spectacular in landscape terms and having the settlements in front of the façade would have been detrimental to the chosen location. In many cases, it would also have been impossible because the church was built right before paddy or river. Therefore the Catholic houses were built behind or beside the church like a flock protected by the shepherd.

I use the word spectacular literally: the location was meant to be theatrical, to attract crowds, to be highly visible. This is the only way to explain what happens with practically all Goan churches, whether they turn their façade to the rising or to the setting sun, are placed before open expanses, large paddy fields, the sudden widening of a river stream, or the explosive view from the top of a hillock. The church always stands white and sovereign dominating the landscape. You see then for miles around, these white façades, and they were white for this purpose, surely, to be seen for miles around, like beacons of the Catholic faith.

Remains of the façade of the old church of Sancoale on the riverbank of the Zuari photographed from a plane approaching Dabolim airport

However, in some Goan towns, the church appears to be located inside the settlement. The more significant case in point is Margão where the Jesuit church faces a very fine *terreiro*-like open space, erroneously, but frequently, referred to as square, which is surrounded by noble houses. Or Chinchinim, where a much larger and less formalized *terreiro* faces the church. Nevertheless, I am persuaded that all of these *terreiros* surrounded by houses appeared late, in the 19th and early 20th centuries. In the early days there was no construction before the church at Margão, Chinchinim and other places.

1

The First Stone Buildings and the Ilhas Type of Churches

One-nave Churches

The Franciscans started building their Order's convent in Old Goa merely 10 years after the conquest of the city, between 1520 and possibly 1527. It was the first convent in Goa and it had the first monastic church in the territory. This church, dedicated to the Holy Spirit (*Espírito Santo*) was a narrow single nave church with lateral chapels, a false transept and a deep chancel. We know this because the original plan of the church was preserved when the building was profoundly remodelled in the 1660s to give origin to the presently existing church.

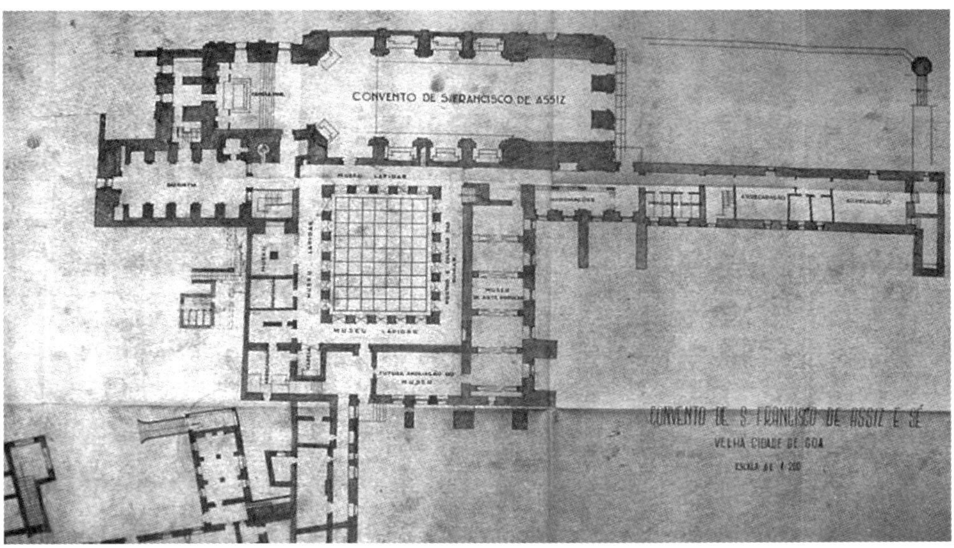

Franciscan convent, Old Goa, plan, detail, Direcção-Geral dos Edifícios e Monumentos Nacionais, Portugal, 1950s

The church had two towers or belfries flanking its chancel judging by the panoramic drawing of Old Goa traced in the *Roteiro* of D. João de Castro dated to c.1536, the earliest known representation of the city. It was to become a common trait of Franciscan churches in Portuguese India, as we shall see, but views of Goa of the late 16th century no longer show these towers.

José Manuel Fernandes (1994) and Nunes Pereira (2005) have demonstrated convincingly that the 17th-century building we now see was founded on the wall structure of the original church. The famous western Manueline portal that appears in so many photographs is not the sole remnant of the early church, as it is normally stated in Goa in naïve repetition of the usual overstatements of late Franciscan chroniclers, nor is it even the more important one.

Among other arguments, Nunes Pereira draws our attention to the peculiar narthex under the choir that we can see in the church's plan (notice the difference in the wall's thickness in this part of the church) and to the proportions of the elongated nave, so different from all 17th-century buildings in Goa and similar to many early 16th-century churches in Portugal and in India (St. Francis in Évora and St. Francis in Cochin, for instance). Furthermore, the existing lateral chapels and their measurements correspond to those found in a letter describing the early church written by its builder Frei António do Louro to the king of Portugal D. Manuel in 1520 (Nunes Pereira 2005: 86).

Most of the churches in Goa maintained this original, very simple, type: they are rectangular single nave buildings with wooden roofs, which were covered at first with palm leaves and later with tiles; at one of the extremities of the nave there is a stone vaulted chancel, the roof of which is lower than the nave's. At the other, a high choir, often built in stone, is raised over the main entrance. These churches have false transepts the only purpose of which is to signify the existence of a cruciform plan and the location of a virtual intersection between the axis from the nave to the chancel and a lateral axis. The altar was frequently located in

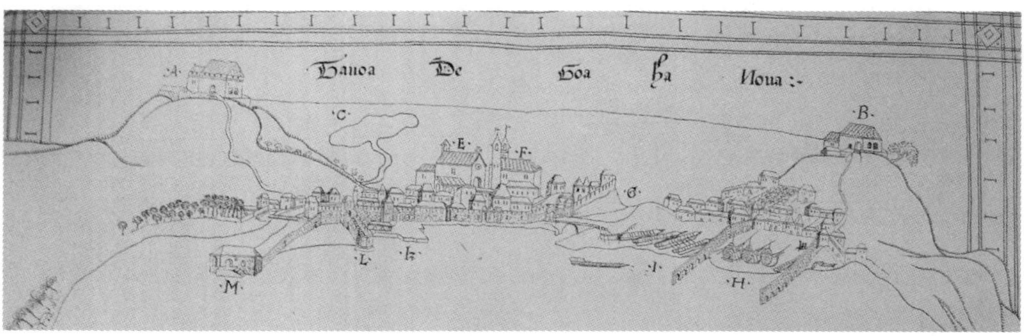

'Tavoa de Goa a Nova' in the 'Roteiro de Goa a Diu' by D. João de Castro, c.1536

this cross separating the stalls for the clergy, which were placed in the chancel, from the laity occupying the nave.

This type of church, the simplest one can imagine and very common in Christian architecture the world over, kept on being built in Goa until the present day. As we shall see, several variations were introduced over time, in particular in what concerns vaulting systems, lateral chapels or niches, and elevated galleries along the nave sides. For these one-nave churches and for the three-nave churches I will discuss in the coming chapter, the early builders devised two types of tower and façade articulations. The nobler was the tower over narthex type of façade.

Tower Over Narthex Façades: *Nossa Senhora do Rosário*

As far as contemporary historiography has been able to ascertain, two Goan churches were built with this type of façade: Santa Catarina (St. Catherine, the first cathedral) and Nossa Senhora do Rosário (Our Lady of the Rosary), both in Velha Goa. To my view, there was a third: Nossa Senhora da Luz (Our Lady of Light).

Santa Catarina was demolished in the 16th century to give way to the presently existing Cathedral. Contemporary descriptions say that it was turned eastward like the existing Cathedral and it had a single tower at the base of which was located a narthex. I will return to this church in the next chapter but this is all we know about its façade.

Nossa Senhora da Luz was one of the earliest churches in Goa, having been founded in the 1540s, together with Rosário, as one of the eight original parishes. It stood over a hill to the south of the city and it has disappeared completely, so much so that even modern drawings or a photographs did not document it. Cottineau de Klogen saw it in the early 19th century, but not Nicolau da Fonseca nor Gabriel de Saldanha. However, a very precise representation exists. It was drawn by Pedro Barreto de Resende (based on previous drawings by Manuel Godinho de Eredia) for the famous report by António Bocarro to the king of Portugal of c.1635 (which was subsequently copied with alterations by other authors). It shows a church with a large three-order high tower over the entrance with all clarity.

De Klogen did not describe the church; indeed he did not describe any of the churches in Goa as he was ignorant of things architectural. But he wrote that 'everything that has been said concerning the church of the Rosary may be applied to this [church]' thus confirming the tower over narthex type.

Nossa Senhora do Rosário is still standing. It is the only European late medieval type of church existing in good condition in the whole of Asia. It is also a truly magnificent building. The history of its construction is yet unclear. In 1548 the chancel was finished and in the

Representation of the church of N.S. da Luz, Old Goa, circa 1635, Pedro Barreto de Resende

N.S. do Rosário, Old Goa, designed between 1515 and 1520, tower over the narthex

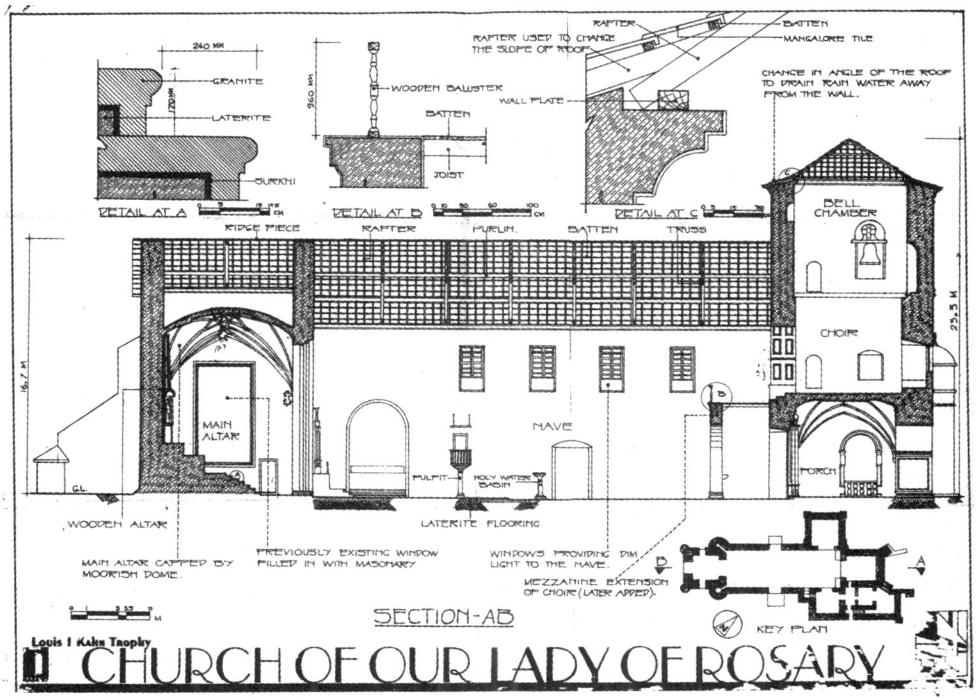

N.S. do Rosário, Old Goa, plan and section, drawing by a group of students of the Goa College of Architecture

subsequent year the walls of the nave were built (Nunes Pereira 2005: 88–93). The only major alteration to the church until the present time seems to have been the dismantling of the wooden ceiling of the nave after part of it collapsed in 1897. The roof now covering the church is modern and there is no ceiling.

Contrary to what has been suggested (Azevedo 1956; Moreira 1995), it does not seem to me that the tower over narthex type adopted by the builders of Rosário was the first in Portuguese India, having inspired all other churches of the same type. I think the first of the kind must have been Santa Catarina in Goa and the church of Santa Cruz (Holy Cross) in Cochin, the parish of the first city in the Indian Ocean where the Portuguese Viceroy resided, founded in 1505 and destroyed in the 17th century, the form of which is shown in a drawing by Pedro Barreto de Resende and in the magnificent panoramic views of Cochin drawn by the Dutch Phillipus Baldeus of the early 1670s. These two churches were built earlier than Rosário.

The tower over narthex type of west front was going through a consistent revival in Portuguese and southwestern Spanish architecture during precisely the early 1500s for reasons to my knowledge not yet discussed by scholars. It is an early-medieval type, the origins of which can be traced to Carolingian architecture at the beginning of the 8th century. Towers over the entrance gave Carolingian churches a fortified appearance – and could indeed function as battlements – but their main purpose was to house a royal tribune over the entrance narthex overlooking the nave.

This type of *westwerk*, the German word commonly used to signify the tower over narthex type of west front, became quite common in the Christian architecture of central Europe, and of the Christian kingdoms of the Asturias in the Iberian Peninsula, during the 9th and 10th centuries. The type was passed on to later times appearing a bit everywhere from 12th-century parish churches in the British Isles to 12th- and 13th-century monastic and Episcopal churches in the south of France. It was the type of west front par excellence of Flemish churches between the 14th and the early 16th centuries and that is undoubtedly why it became popular again in Portugal and Spain at this later epoch, given the close economic and cultural ties then existing between the Iberian Peninsula and Flanders.

In Portugal, two very important medieval churches of the 12th century had already adopted the tower over narthex type of west front: the priories of Coimbra (Santa Cruz) and Lisboa (S.Vicente), both royal foundations for the order of St.Augustine. Neither exists in its original form, which is only known to us by descriptions and archaeological soundings in the case of Coimbra and by 16th-century drawings in the case of Lisboa.

In the early 16th century, king D. Manuel (r. 1496-1521) patronized a profound intervention in Santa Cruz, Coimbra in order to remodel its interior where the mausolea of Portugal's first two kings D. Afonso Henriques and D. Sancho I were placed since the origin of the monarchy in the 12th century. In the course of these works a new façade was built, modernizing yet retaining the tower over narthex type.

In late medieval and early modern Europe, tower over narthexes were used to house high choirs over the western entrance. This was a logical outcome of the choice of the type, where the tower was originally designed to house a royal tribune. Even more so in Portugal where practically all churches, either in convents or parishes, had choirs over the entrance built or adapted since the end of the 15th century, the time of D. Manuel. The high choir became a typical characteristic of Portuguese churches although it exists in some other European regions (but not many).

D. Manuel liked to see himself and to have himself seen as a direct heir of Portugal's founding kings, first because he was no such thing, but only a member of a collateral branch of the dynasty, and second because the opening of the sea route to India in 1498 was seen in his close circle of courtiers as the first step to a Christian world empire and Portugal as a monarchy that would have been destined to found it (Thomaz 1994).

It should also be remembered, and D. Manuel's court circles certainly had this fact in mind, that both Santa Cruz in Coimbra and S. Vicente in Lisbon had been founded by Portugal's first king D. Afonso Henriques. They were monuments to the foundation of the kingdom and to Christian Crusade. Lisbon's church was built immediately after the city was conquered from the Moors by the king in 1147 as a sign of the triumph of the monarchy and of Christianity. A symbolic re-foundation of the Portuguese monarchy in a Crusade context was the order of the day at the time of D. Manuel and the complete remodelling of Santa Cruz in Coimbra should perhaps be seen within this set of ideas.

The type entered India at precisely the same epoch when it was becoming popular in Portugal and it triumphed in India probably because it stood for the ideas of Crusade and Christian monarchy in Manueline circles. In fact, Santa Catarina in Goa and Santa Cruz in Cochin (the name is certainly no coincidence, echoing the church at Coimbra) shared the same urban and religious dignity: they were the respective town's main Catholic temples and, in this sense, they were founding churches of the two more important Portuguese settlements in India. In addition, and to my view significantly, the type was adopted in 1547 for the parish church of the capital of the North, Baçaim (Bassein), the church of S. José (St. Joseph), and maybe also for the parish of Diu located in the fort (the church has long disappeared but is represented in a drawing by Gaspar Correa).

Detail of the representation of Diu in "Lendas da Índia" by Gaspar Correa, ca. 1530

Church of Madalena, Olivença, Spain, begun 1510, tower over narthex

Church of Elvas, Portugal, ca. 1517

Church of Atalaia, Portugal, founded 1528

Parish church of Pedrógão Grande, Portugal, concluded 1537

After Santa Cruz in Coimbra, many tower over narthex churches were built at D. Manuel's time and immediately after, especially in southeast Portugal along the border with Spain. On the other side of this border, a series of churches of the exact same type were then founded in Estremadura and western Andalucia. I am not aware of any study that has discussed these facts that are obviously not coincidental.

The Portuguese frontier churches were the parishes of Olivença (begun 1510) and Elvas, later Cathedral (1517). In central Portugal, in the area of influence of the Order of Christ whose links with the King and the sea faring enterprise are well known, the examples are the church of Atalaia founded by the noble family of the Cantanhedes in 1528, the parish churches of Pedrogão Grande (1537) and of Areias (1548).

The tower over narthex was chosen for Rosário in Goa probably because of its novelty but more likely because of the building's very special location atop the westernmost hill of Old Goa, facing the setting sun and the river route that every ship had to take approaching or leaving the city. The massive tower of Rosário became Old Goa's symbolic gate, its primary

Parish church of Areias, Portugal, concluded 1548

View of N.S. do Rosário from the Mandovi river

tower, the first building one sees when arriving, the last when departing. When D. João de Castro himself designed the earliest known view of Old Goa in c.1536, the new capital of the Portuguese in India appears in the drawing solidly framed by its two Marian shrines, its spiritual fortresses: Our Lady of the Mount to the East, Our Lady of Rosary to the West, both founded by Albuquerque. Our Lady of Light, to the south, also built on a hill, was Old Goa's third Marian gate.

It is usually assumed that Rosário was begun in the early 1540s because the parishioners, when they asked the king for money to finish the church in 1549, said that they had completely demolished an original church which would have been built during Afonso de Albuquerque's time (r. 1509–15) and under his command, and that the chancel of the new church had been begun 'in past years' (Nunes Pereira 2005: 89).

However, 'past years' (*anos passados*) does not necessarily mean 'recent years'. Second, the claim that an extant church was 'completely demolished' is a convenient excuse to get more funding (and one frequently used). Third, on stylistic grounds it is unlikely that the church's chancel was begun in the 1540s. I would definitely suggest that the overall design of the church was done in Albuquerque's time.

It has been frequently observed that Rosário is a transitional church in stylistic terms exhibiting both late-medieval and Renaissance forms. This is of course true and it means that it was designed and built at a time when the taste of patrons and builders was shifting from one type of forms to the other: the late 1520s, the 1530s and 1540s in the Portuguese influenced world.

The type of the church, its single nave with a tower over narthex, is not only late-medieval but, as we have seen, characteristic of a particular south Portuguese and south-western Spanish circumstance of the first three decades of the 16th century. Furthermore, the vaults covering Rosário's chancel, its south lateral chapel and the narthex, the rope mouldings along the outside cornices of the tower, the solomonic columns embedded in the four corners of the tower's upper story, are all typical of Portuguese Manueline, i.e., of Portuguese architecture between 1500 and 1520. This must be when Rosário was designed and its foundations laid, maybe when its chancel and the tower were built. There is no logical reason to assume a 20- or 30-year stylistic lag between what happened in Portugal and in Portuguese India. When, in the 1540s and 1550s, building resumed after an interval of maybe one or two decades, Renaissance taste was introduced in Rosário: the mouldings of the frontal and side doors and the dome of the little baptistery under the north turret are typical of that style.

N.S. do Rosário, Old Goa, chancel

N.S. do Rosário, Old Goa, frontal door, detail

These Renaissance elements in Rosário, that have been described by Rafael Moreira, with some reason, as 'pure copies' of the sculptural work of the church of Graça in Évora of the 1530s (Moreira:1995), are of the same type as that of the door frame of S. José of Bassein's lateral eastern door, one of the earliest surviving elements of that church begun in 1546.

S. José, Baçaim, begun 1546, view from the ruins of the nave

S. José in Bassein, the other Indian church of the same type to have reached the present times in recognizable form, has a completely different tower from Rosário because it was designed later: Rosário's tower is square, massive, flanked by beautiful cylindrical buttresses that house, one a spiral staircase to the choir on the tower's first story, the other the baptistery. Its sisters in proportion in the Iberian Peninsula are the tower of Olivença and the one of Pedrogão Grande (albeit none as beautiful as Rosário's and none accompanied by cylindrical turrets). Bassein's tower is different: slender, rectangular in plan, it has separated bell towers located to its flanks and looks much more like the Renaissance towers of Spanish churches or of Elvas. Be as it may, Nossa Senhora do Rosário is an outstanding building, the most beautiful early Portuguese church in India, the only expressive architectural masterpiece to have survived more or less intact from early Portuguese Goa.

One Tower, Steep Gable Façade Churches

Another type of west front for single nave churches was created in early times: one bay façades crowned by a very steep gable, having a single low and massive tower placed to one of the sides, frequently slightly behind the façade. I believe this was one of the earliest types of west front for Portuguese churches all over India from the moment these began being built in stone, covered with proper roofs and provided with a vaulted chancel. This is perhaps documented by two facts. First, in regions where later types were not introduced because church architecture did not evolve, like the former *Província do Norte*, this type of west front can still be seen in many churches in spite of 19th-century ornamental alterations. Second, in Goa, the type exists almost exclusively in Ilhas and this probably means that it is indeed an early form, having been experimented with when Christianity was limited to this region before it spread with Portuguese dominion to Salcete and Bardez.

Judging by the dates available, the churches with this type of west front were founded in Ilhas over a long period ranging from the 1540s to the early 17th century: S. Miguel Arcanjo (St. Micael the Archangel) in Taleigão, a Dominican priory, was founded in 1544; the parish church of S. Pedro (St. Peter) in Penelim was founded by the Viceroy in 1545 and built by masons from Portugal. The church of Santa Luzia (Saint Lucia), in the then very important parish of the same invocation located to the southeast of Old Goa, was also founded around 1544; it was demolished in 1873 (Saldanha 1926: 20–21) and is known only through a drawing by Lopes Mendes. The church of S. Brás (St. Blaise), a parish that incorporated Santa Luzia in 1846, is similar as regards façade and tower type. Nossa Senhora da Ajuda (Our Lady of Help) in Ribandar was already in existence in 1554 (Bragança Pereira 1945) and S. Lourenço (St.Lawrence) at Agaçaim was begun in 1565. The last church in the series, S. João Facundo at Corlim, was built in the early 17th century.

S. Miguel Arcanjo, Taleigão, founded 1544

S. Pedro, Penelim, founded 1545

Santa Luzia, demolished 1873, drawing pub. by Lopes Mendes, 1886

N. S. da Ajuda, Ribandar, founded ca. 1550

S. Lourenço, Agaçaim, beg. 1565, porch late 20th century

S. João, Corlim, early 17th century

These churches are located in what were at the time very important parishes outside Old Goa: the aristocratic suburbs of Penelim and Ribandar, the rich agricultural fields of Taleigão and Corlim and, in the case of Agaçaim, the main passage from Ilhas to Salcete across the Zuari river. It is possible that other churches in the whereabouts of Old Goa, namely at Carambolim and what are now Santa Cruz and Mercês, had the same type of west front and this was later replaced by the presently existing façades. The Franciscan church of Nerul in southwestern Bardez, founded in 1569 but probably built in its present form in the early 17th century is of this type but without the tower (it has two belfries which, together with the decoration of the façade and the porch, seem to be 19th-century works.

The only church of the series that is not located in Ilhas is Nossa Senhora dos Mártires (Our Lady of the Martyrs) at Assolna, Salcete. According to several sources quoted by the local historian Sacramento de Almeida, the church was founded circa 1590 in the 'ruins' of a fortification that existed there since at least 1583 (Almeida 1958: 67). In fact, the church is located at the bank of a tributary of river Sal, at a place where a fort could very well have stood. The church's nave is substantially different from all the others in this series: it is wider and it has two rows of windows, thus seeming to correspond to a later construction. This leads me to think that the Jesuits made use of the tower and frontal wall of an early church that would have existed at the fort to build their own church in 1590.

N.S. dos Remédios, Nerul, founded 1569

N.S. dos Mártires, Assolná, founded ca. 1590

These churches were all without exception extensively built or rebuilt in the late 16th or the early 17th century but the steep gable frontal façades were retained. In the *Província do Norte* many churches built *ex novo* in the last years of the 16th century have adopted this type of façade. The sharp silhouette of all the churches in Daman is a particularly obvious case but one can see the same type of gable throughout *Salsete do Norte* (the Salsete area of present-day metropolitan Mumbai) and in the area of Bassein. Even the demolished churches once located in what is now the city of Mumbai and later replaced by modern buildings, known to us only by photographs (Glory in Mazgaon, Salvação in Dadar) kept this type of gable in spite of extensive modifications in the 18th and 19th centuries. These cases prove that the type was indeed successful.

In the interiors and in many doors of the churches of Taleigão, Penelim, Agaçaim, Ribandar, Nerul, Corlim and Assolna we can see elements of the exact same type: mouldings composed of one or two frames sculpted into the shafts of pilasters and into arches. This type of ornament also appears in the late 16th-century or early 17th-century buildings of Old Goa, in particular the remains of the façade of S. Paulo, dated from the late 1560s (see both the photographs of the façade's ruins by Sousa & Paul and the remains in situ), in the Bom Jesus church (see the triumphal arch, the chancel's vault coffers, the nave pilasters, and so on), at Santa Mónica, at the church of the Augustinians (see the arches leading to the cloister), at

Salvação, Dadar, Bombay (demolished), photo published 1925

S. Lourenço, Agaçaim, detail of the upper choir support

Our Lady of The Mount (main arch, false transept), and at the Cathedral (transept chapels). This seems to confirm that the churches being discussed here were indeed built or rebuilt in their present form at this time.

The inclination of the roof gable is the most conspicuous element of this type of church. Nowadays it no longer corresponds to the roof inclination, as both roof slopes are lower. But it was not so in the past, as one can see looking at these gables from behind: the former roof supports are still visible in some cases, showing that old roofs were much steeper than subsequent ones (although never as steep as the gable; the inclination was due to stylistic reasons more than utility).

I haven't yet found a satisfying explanation for why these roofs were built. Old images and many preserved buildings prove that steep roofs were common in Medieval and Early Modern Europe, including in Portugal where some such roofs have survived (see the *Sala de Actos* of Coimbra's University, of the mid-17th century). Perhaps the type of tiles then used throughout Europe (flat ceramic or slate tiles) and the type of tiles used along Asia's coasts, demanded a steep roof slope. And perhaps when modern tiles appeared in European construction, roofs had to change.

S. João, Corlim, interior towards the altar

The churches at Ilhas and Nerul are single nave buildings devoid of side chapels. They have long and low bodies covered by a wooden roof, and a stone vaulted box-like chancel to the east. Most have stone-built high-choirs over the entrance with the exception of Ribandar where there is only a wooden choir.

S. João, Corlim, views of the tower articulation, south and north

High placed rectangular windows appear along the naves of Penelim, Taleigão and Ribandar, which constitutes an early solution (one can see it at Rosário), although the windows at Taleigão have been transformed in the 19th century and their presence inside the church is now disguised by modern wooden galleries running along both sides of the nave. Agaçaim has two rows of windows and Corlim a single row placed at 'normal' height.

The churches at Penelim, Taleigão, S. Brás, Agaçaim and Ribandar have massive towers placed to the north of their frontal façades. In the case of Corlim the tower is to the south and it was not built at the same time as the rest of the church or its frontal façade with which it has no correct architectural articulation. Just compare the awkward way in which the cornices of the tower and the northern wall meet with the very elegant cornice that connects the frontal façade and the wall on the south side. I propose that the tower was already there when the body of the church was built or enlarged because the opposite is much less likely: I can think of no reason why builders would make a mess of the simple job of building a new tower for an older building. Using an old tower when renovating a building makes a lot more sense, especially a good, solid, square tower like the one still standing at Corlim.

Penelim, Agaçaim, Ribandar and Corlim all have false transepts, not S. Miguel de Taleigão but this exception could be the result of modern changes. Teleigão, Ribandar, Agaçaim and Corlim (and Nerul) have the same type of barrel vaults covering their chancels, decorated (and

N.S. da Ajuda, Ribandar, false transept

made lighter) by square coffers. Corlim's chancel is dated and signed *in situ*, a very uncommon fact in the history of Portuguese architecture. Engraved in the lower stone step of the main altar, with a fine moulding of rosettes, we can read, at the left side:

esta obr[a] *fez alexo frz* [this work was done by Aleixo Fernandes]

The fact that the inscription was chiselled in the stone step and not in the altar shows that Aleixo Fernandes, of whom I know nothing else, was responsible for the building (and the design) of the chancel itself. Since all the architectural mouldings in the chancel are exactly like those of the high choir and doors, we may conclude that Aleixo Fernandes designed the whole church and not just the chancel. The stone step at the right side of the base of the altar bears the rest of the inscription and it contains a date, unfortunately mutilated at its crucial digits as it often happens in order to allow for legend to flourish as to the real age of buildings:

no anno d... 1 ? ?(3 or 8) 4

My reading of the date is 1634. The mouldings of all the arches in the interior correspond to this date, not to the other possible readings, 1534 or 1584, which would be both too early. In 1534, mouldings such as those in the church did not exist in Goa. As for 1584, the reasoning that leads me to discard this date is more complex: the church is dedicated to S. João Facundo or S. João de Sahagun, a Spaniard beatified by Augustinian influence at an uncertain date between 1572 and 1601 and canonized in 1592. The image of the Saint still adorns the altar (not S. Lázaro – ST. Lazarus – as erroneously published and repeated). In 1592, a very important Augustinian church at Porto, in Portugal, changed its invocation to S. João Facundo (the church is popularly known as S. João Novo). Corlim's church was Augustinian, it was founded by the Augustinian Archbishop D. frei Aleixo de Menezes (1596–1609), but it was not built during his time because the Jesuit chronicle by Sebastião Gonçalves, of 1614, does not mention its existence when it lists the works by the Archbishop (Bragança Pereira 1947: 8). In 1616 an altar of S. João de Sahagun was inaugurated at the Augustinian's mother church in Old Goa, N.S. da Graça (Our Lady of Grace) (Vítor Serrão 2008).

The date 1684 is also impossible because the chancel's barrel vault was no longer fashionable in Goa at that time. As we shall see later in the book, from the 1660s onwards Goan architects built another kind of vault, one we can also see at Corlim but at the Holy Sacrament chapel: a planed vault with penetrations for the windows. This chapel is dated, now with all digits clearly visible, in a tombstone containing the remains of the chapel's founder, Francisco de Aguiar, and the date is 1716 (incidentally, a Sacrament chapel of this type was also built at Agaçaim, opening to the southern flank of the nave). Therefore what I think happened in Corlim is that the church was completely built or rebuilt in 1634 and in 1716 the Holy Sacrament chapel was added.

The vault of S. Pedro de Penelim's chancel is also new, of the same type as Corlim's Sacrament chapel and of roughly the same period. The church of Santa Inês in Panjim, rebuilt in 1605 by D. frei Aleixo, could be yet another church in this series: its façade recalls the early type with its steep gable, one tower and one simple belfry.

The façades of S. Pedro de Penelim, S. Miguel de Taleigão, Nossa Senhora da Ajuda de Ribandar, the disappeared Santa Luzia and S. Brás, are protected by porches, but not the façades at Agaçaim and Corlim (the porches we see there are very recent). These porches were all built later than the original façades as we can easily ascertain by observing the way the builders had to cut through existing window and door mouldings to instal them. Porches were probably made necessary as the number of people attending masses on special occasions increased. But this alone does not explain why windows and doors were at first

Santa Inês, Panjim, rebuilt 1605

not protected with lasting architectural devices. The patrons of the initial churches were obviously not counting on the tropical sun and the torrencial rains of the monsoon, and, peculiarly enough, they seemed to stubbornly disregard these climatic conditions until the present times, preferring to protect the doors and windows of the churches with temporary devices made of palm tree leaves (and in modern times with corrugated metal sheet) than to imagine original designs for their façades.

Some porches, like the ones at Penelim and Ribandar are probably almost as old as the original façades. In Pedro Barreto de Resende's drawings of the 1630s we can already see a few churches dotted with porches that look very much like the one at Penelim. On the contrary, the simple three-arch porches used in S. Luzia, Nerul and many Franciscan churches in Bardez, to which I will come back later in this book, are likely later in date than the original façades. Complex porches like the one protecting Taleigão's façade probably came much later.

Unlike the mouldings at all other churches, the main door and the northern lateral door at S. Pedro are typical experimental Renaissance forms of the 1540s or 1550s, a fact that seems to indicate that this might be the church which has maintained more of the early architectural characteristics.

One tower, steep-gabled façade churches were the earliest parish churches built in stone in Goa. The systematic presence of the towers – almost always massive and almost without openings – could indicate that these churches could also be used to shelter people in case of Bijapuri raids, which were frequent until the end of the 16th century.

2

The Churches in the *Cidade de Goa*

Three Nave Churches

In the first 40 years of Portuguese rule in the city of Goa, from 1510 to 1550, only four religious buildings of considerable dimensions were built in stone: the Franciscan convent with its church of Espírito Santo, the church of Nossa Senhora do Rosário, the church of N. S. da Luz, all already discussed in this book, and the parish church, later Cathedral, of Santa Catarina, the patron Saint of the city (Goa was conquered on the day of this Saint, 25 November 1510).

The type chosen by frei Domingos de Sousa, vicar-general of India, for Santa Catarina, since as early as 1514, was a roof-covered three-nave church with a three chapel stone vaulted chevet and a transept. As we already know it had a single tower over narthex type of façade like the other early churches (Nunes Pereira 2005: 80–81). The plan was fairly common in Portugal and throughout the whole of Europe since at least the 13th century because it addressed the requirements of preaching to large congregations in the central nave and of the simultaneous existence of aisles and lateral chapels where other functions could take place.

The building is known only through descriptions because it was demolished in the 16th century in order to give way to a more modern church, especially since it became the Cathedral after the creation of Goa's diocese in 1532. For instance, we don't even know whether the original roof was supported, and the three naves separated, by pillars or columns.

In the 1550s and 1560s, two large architectural enterprises exerted a major influence in the city: the convent and church of the Dominicans and the college and church of the Jesuits. Both churches were three-nave buildings, definitely a prestigious type in mid-sixteenth century Old Goa. The convent church of the Dominicans, one of the largest and richest in Goa, was begun around 1550 and concluded in 1564 (Ibid.: 101 ff). The design came from Lisbon brought by the first Dominican friars in 1548.

Two drawings by Lopes Mendes, a side view of the main façade and part of the nave and a bird's eye view of the ruins of the convent in a panoramic view of Old Goa copied from a drawing by another author unknown to us, show that the church's tower was located at the

Ruins of the church and convent of S. Domingos, Old Goa, pub. Lopes Mendes 1886

side of the chancel and that several chapels of different plans and heights were added to the church's naves throughout the centuries. The convent had three courtyards. A large one to the north of the church was certainly a cloister. A large staircase existed before the façade.

The church was praised throughout the times as one of the architectural masterpieces of Goa. The façade and some ruins still existed in the 1850s but all was gone in 1873 when the *Sketch of the City of Goa* by José Nicolau da Fonseca was published. The cross seen in Lopes Mendes drawing still exists *in situ,* and some people still apply the name Rua (street) de S. Domingos to the road where the convent and church stood for centuries and where one now sees a couple of uninteresting modern houses among coconut trees and unkempt alleys. The church had no choir over the entrance but only a large friars' choir in the chancel. We are aware of this detail and not of more important features because Cottineau de Klogen took due notice that this was unusual in Portuguese churches.

It is almost certain that the twelve Composite (not Corinthian) columns of Bassein basalt that sustain the Doric entablature and the cupola of the Monument to Afonso de Albuquerque raised in Pangim's main square in 1847, did indeed come from the church as indicated by several Goan sources. They separated the three naves of the church, six per row, probably supporting the arches that sustained the roof.

We are better informed about the Jesuit church (Ibid.: 115 ff) but the essential facts still evade us as is the case of the Dominican convent. The first Jesuit church in Old Goa was dedicated to S. Paulo in 1541 and located at the Rua da Carreira dos Cavalos (street for the training of horses) in the eastern outskirts of the city. It belonged to the already existing Seminary of Santa Fé and probably was a very modest palm-covered building.

The definitive buildings, those that would last until the 19th century, were started in 1560 and the church was concluded circa 1573. The three naves of the church were separated, and the wooden roof was supported, by Doric columns, a more sober choice than the Composite adopted by the Dominicans. The three chapels in the chevet were covered by coffered barrel vaults. Sometime in the late 1560s the Jesuits decided to vault the entire church but construction was stopped in 1581 after cracks in the vaults and walls were detected. The four famous arches that gave the church its name of S. Paulo dos Arcos (of the arches) were added to the northern façade over the Rua da Carreira dos Cavalos (the southern flank of the church did not need buttressing because it was protected by the Seminary's building).

All that remains of S. Paulo besides images (the more important being two façade photographs by Sousa & Paul), are the ruins of the façade inscribed in the unbelievably ridiculous object-trouvé type of monument that we see at the site. However, a British officer stationed in Goa in the early 19th century made a drawing of the church as it still stood

Ruins of the church of S. Paulo, Old Goa, 1560-1581, photo Sousa & Paul, late 19th century

S. Paulo, Old Goa, drawing of the early 19th cenury, British Library

then, which was recently made available online by the British Library. It shows what the upper part of the façade looked like then—but not necessarily how it was designed and built originally. In fact, this image probably shows the aspect of the church after the vault of the central nave was dismantled. Judging by the neoclassical expression of the central top element it could even show a very late attempt at reconstituting the façade.

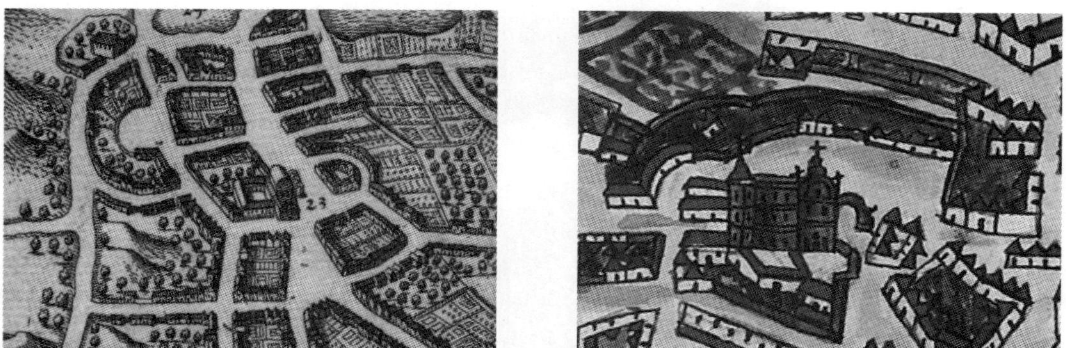

Representations of S. Paulo, Old Goa, according to Linschoten (pub. 1596) – 40a – and Pedro Barreto de Resende (ca. 1635) – 40b

Jesuit church, Baçaim, concluded 1636

There are, however, trustworthy representations of S. Paulo's exterior in the transition between the 16th and the 17th centuries: Linschoten's panorama of Old Goa and Pedro Barreto de Resende's drawing. They both show a church covered with an exposed hemispherical dome, that is, with no roof, and with a corresponding semi-circular topped façade. This type of façade was replicated at the Jesuit church of Bassein, rebuilt at the beginning of the 17th century. It is highly uncommon in European architecture: there are some cases in 15th- and 16th-century Venice, but not many more.

Of course, Bassein has only one nave whereas Goa had three. The curved top was probably narrower than the full width of the façade, as suggested by architect Sidh Losa Mendiratta with whom I have discussed this hypothesis. In any case, here lies the origin of the vertically placed rectangle type of façade that the Jesuits favoured in India and that we sill see at the Bom Jesus, at Diu, and at Bassein.

The existing remains of the church's portal and the photographs by Sousa & Paul allow us to speculate on some formal elements that the Jesuit façade, probably completed in 1573, would have contributed to subsequent Goan architecture. The frames sculpted into the

S. Paulo, Old Goa, possible aspect of original façade, drawing by Sidh Losa Mendiratta

shafts of the pilasters that we can see on the façade's lateral bays were immensely popular throughout Goa from then on. The ornamental motives over the niches and over the central and lateral upper windows are also remarkable because they are of the same kind of those that later appear in Jesuit façades throughout Salcete, namely in Verná, Loutolim, Majordá and others.

As for the overall *parti* of the façade's doorway, with its altar-like design, the Jesuits have favoured it in their more important Indian foundations of the second half of the 16th century, the more noteworthy of which is the church of Bassein, of the same type as S. Paulo's: a main door framed by two pairs of Corinthian columns placed against a stone plane articulated by Doric pilasters, a window above it and a round oculus on top. The same composition can also be seen at the main church of Daman probably designed by a Jesuit architect.

The New Cathedral

While the Jesuits were building their church, the remodelling began in 1562 of Santa Catarina in order to transform it into a worthy Cathedral for the Bishop of all Catholics east of Mozambique. The Cathedral of Goa is part of a series. In 50 years, between 1550 and

1600, seven new Cathedrals, corresponding to seven new dioceses, were added to the 10 that existed until that time in Portugal, eight founded in the Middle Ages, one in the 15th century (Guarda) and another at the beginning of the 16th (Funchal). The new Cathedrals were, in chronological order, Leiria, Portalegre and Miranda-do-Douro in Europe, Goa in India, Angra at the Azores, Salvador da Baía in Brazil (demolished in the early 20th century), and Ribeira Grande in the archipelago of Cape Verde (now in ruins). The three Cathedrals in Portugal were designed between 1549 and 1554, construction began between 1554 and 1559, the chevets were ready between 1566 and 1570 (precisely the years during which the building of Goa began) and the buildings, except Goa, were concluded between 1574 and the end of the century.

Comparing the plans of all the Cathedrals to the same scale one realizes two things: the first and more striking is that Goa's is by far the largest. But then again all churches in the city of Goa are larger than most Portuguese churches of the 16th and 17th centuries and, as the purpose of the Cathedrals was none other than to accommodate all the faithful of the Bishop's parish in festive days, and as Goans certainly outnumbered the parishioners of Leiria, Portalegre and Miranda put together, it is no wonder that Goa's Cathedral is gigantic.

The second aspect that the comparison between the Cathedrals brings to our attention is the obvious typological similarity between the plans of the first four buildings: Leiria, Portalegre, Miranda and Goa. They all have a double square plan, i.e., a plan generated by the joining of two squares. All have three naves separated by pillars. Goa and Portalegre have lateral chapels running along the side naves. Very large main chapels, as long as one-third of the nave's length, appear at Leiria and Goa (Miranda's main chapel is from the 18th century and we don't know the form of the original chevet).

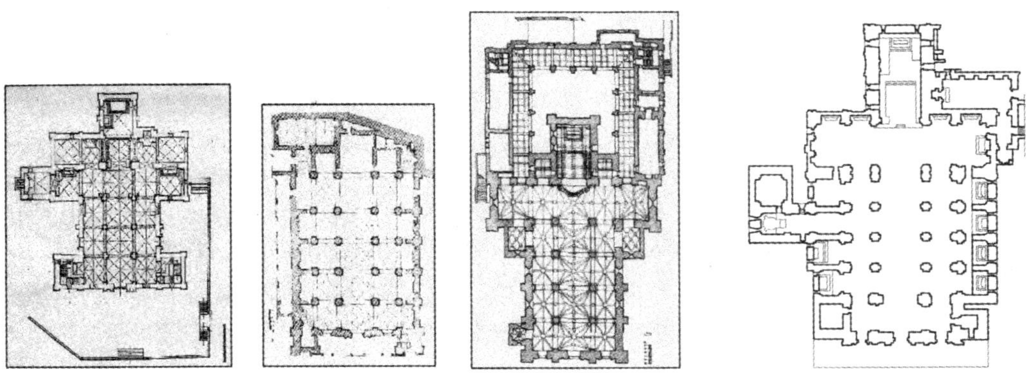

Plans of the Cathedrals of Miranda do Douro, Portalegre, Leiria and Goa to the same scale (Lúcia Figueiredo, 2001)

Of all the scholars who have written on the evolution of the Cathedral's construction, António Nunes Pereira has taken further a comprehensive discussion of the problems that the building presents in the absence of written documents clarifying the successive periods of the works (2005: 139 ff; 181 ff). However, I don't agree with his more important conclusion: that the Cathedral's essential built elements, from the plan to the vaults, result from the original mid-sixteenth-century design. I tend to see the complicated process of the Sé's building more along the lines of Pedro Dias' reasoning (2003 and 2005): there was a fundamental change in the design of supports and vaults in the early 17th century.

The basic known facts about the chronology of the works are the following: The royal order coming from Lisbon to have a new Sé replace the early one arrived in Goa in 1562 and the foundations of the Cathedral must have been laid in the following years. With Nunes Pereira, I am convinced that the plan that was respected to the end is the original one. It probably came from Lisbon, traced, like Leiria's, Portalegre's and Miranda's, by the King's architects and then adapted to local conditions by the architects active in Goa, maybe Inofre de Carvalho (act. 1551–68), as first suggested by Rafael Moreira (1995).

After that, throughout the 1570s, 1580s and 1590s, following the financial, political and military crisis that crippled the *Estado da Índia*, the construction was stalled. Only with the intervention of the Viceroy D. Francisco da Gama (1597–1600) did things change. In 1596, King Philip II of Portugal (Philip III of Spain) had acknowledged a piece of information from the Archbishop that the cost and delays in the completion of the work derived from the fact that the Sé was large, its walls were thick and had many 'sculpted stones both inside and outside'. The Archbishop's words do not necessarily mean that the Cathedral then under construction was a very rich building. They could simply signify that, at the time, there were virtually no richly decorated buildings under construction in Goa (with the exception of the Jesuit Professed House of the Bom Jesus) and that the Archbishop valued the Cathedral against a background of general poverty.

D. Francisco arrived in Goa in 1597 and, in the manner of a Renaissance Prince, he brought as part of his personal retinue an architect: the name this architect was known by in Goa was Júlio Simão. He was to change the panorama of Goan architecture. Besides travelling with D. Francisco to serve him personally, Simão also carried the more important royal appointment to India: he was chief engineer of the *Estado*, succeeding the Italian Giovanni Battista Cairato who had left India in 1596. In the official document the King calls Simão *meu moço de câmara* (my chamber attendant), a position normally reserved for *fidalgos* or men specially favoured by the King.

Simão did his first work not for the King but for the Viceroy: he designed the so-called Arch of the Viceroys, in fact a monument commissioned by D. Francisco in commemoration of his grandfather Vasco da Gama and of the first centenary of the arrival of the Portuguese in India in 1498. It was a princely commission and a typical Renaissance gesture. Simão probably brought the design with him from Europe, or at least the general idea of the monument. It had no precedent in Portuguese architectural culture, nor does the Arch recall any previously existing Portuguese building. Its prototypes are classically Roman and its design comes from Italian treatises like the one by Sebastiano Serlio's (from 1537 to 1551) and others.

The Arch today stands as an isolated construction since the Viceroy's palace in Old Goa was demolished in the 19th century. However, it was originally not a Triumphal Arch but a decorated monumental archway that passed under an important wing of the Palace, where the Viceroy's audience hall stood. It was one of the main gates of Goa since pre-Portuguese times and it became the *Porta do Mar* (Sea Gate) typical of all Portuguese settlements by the sea, leading to the city's more important thoroughfares. Simão signed the Arch in Latin: *IVLIVS SIMON ING. MAG. INV.* (Julius Simon Chief Engineer has Done This Work), again a very uncommon gesture in Portuguese architectural culture.

Following the work on the Arch, he must have taken charge of the Cathedral's construction because one of the towers in the western façade was completed during the years of D. Francisco da Gama's government, and this can only mean that the walls had attained sufficient height all around the church's perimeter and the façade was being built. Immediately after this, in the early years of the 17th century, works seem to have stopped again. We know that all construction in Goa was blocked then, including the fortifications: fort Aguada, fort Gaspar Dias, the wall surrounding the *Velha Cidade* and its territory. The years from 1600

Model of the Vice Roy's palace, Old Goa, designed by architect Hélder Carita (Museu do Oriente, Lisbon)

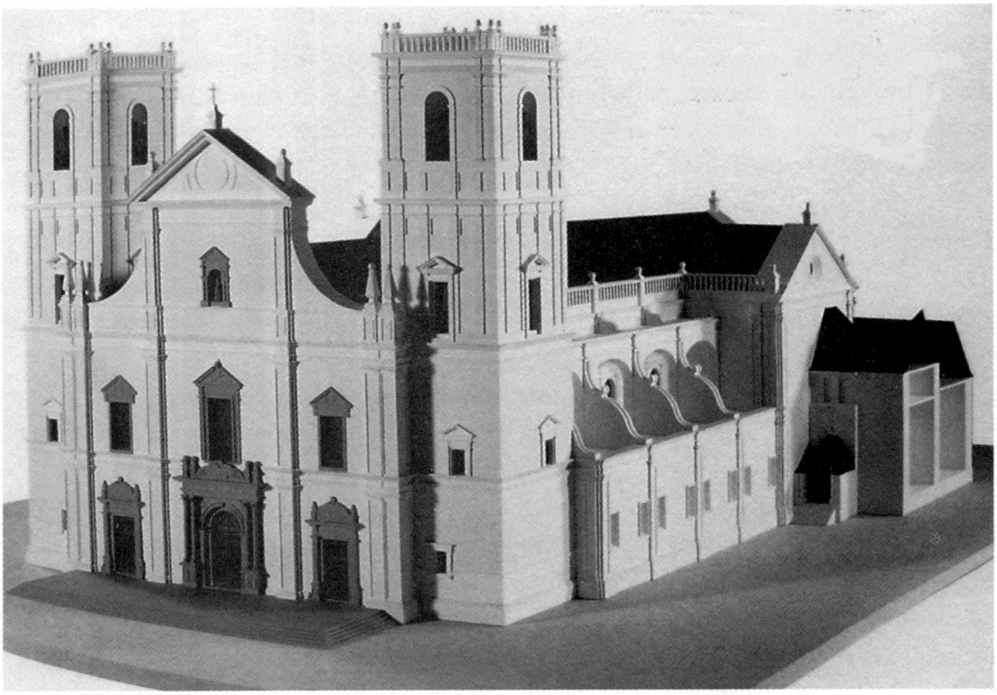

Cathedral, Old Goa, completed 1630–1634, model with original towers (Museu do Oriente, Lisbon)

to 1610 were difficult years for the *Estado da Índia* with the imminent threat posed by the Dutch and a severe financial crisis.

In 1620, seemingly all of a sudden, written sources tell us that the naves of the Cathedral were concluded. In the period 1625–29 the crossing and the chancel were built, the façade and towers were finished between 1630 and 1634, the main altar was commissioned to Simão by Viceroy Linhares in 1630 (V. Serrão 2008) and the Cathedral was considered completed (although works continued until 1652).

When Júlio Simão died he was buried at the Cathedral's crossing and the epitaph, which he himself undoubtedly devised, reads: *mestre arquitecto das obras desta Sé* (master architect of this See's works), yet another thing totally unexpected in Portuguese architecture: no architect had ever done that or would do so in the centuries to come. Moreover, it was certainly true. The spate of building activity in the Cathedral after 1597 and especially in the 1620s and 1630s, and the fact that these works were the completion of the whole building from chancel to towers mean that, apart from the plan, everything having to do with architectural articulation in the Cathedral, every order, every moulding, every ornament was designed by Júlio Simão. The design decisions about the vaulting system of the building too were, according to me, made by him.

The Sé is a false basilica, as described by Nunes Pereira. His discussion of the building's type in comparison to other Portuguese Cathedrals deserves to be cited in full:

> Much more than the similarities between the plans of Goa and Portalegre, the differences between these two buildings are what matters in what concerns the internal space and the articulation of façades and walls. If we closely observe the four Cathedrals [Leiria, Portalegre, Miranda and Goa] we easily conclude that Goa differs more from its Portuguese counterparts than these amongst themselves. Whilst the Portuguese Cathedrals are *hallenkirchen*, Goa is a false basilica. This is not just about the naves' height, which is not so different in Goa, but about space configuration. In Goa we don't see homogeneous and continuous internal space produced by similar arches between bays and between central and lateral naves, or the fusion of space units (naves and transept) that characterizes Portuguese Cathedrals. In Goa, all space units are clearly defined and separated. The barrel vaults over the naves, contrary to groin vaults, possess clear directional thrust, thus highlighting the longitudinal arrangement of the

Cathedral, Old Goa, interior towards the main altar

Cathedral of Leiria, Portugal, interior in a late 19th century photo

Cathedral along the central and lateral naves. This is reinforced by the round arches between naves, placed longitudinally on rectangular pillars, not square like in the other Cathedrals. The lateral naves do not merge into the transept space as in the Portuguese *Sés*, but are separated from it by lower arches. Unlike what happens in Portalegre, lateral chapels are separated from the naves by deep double arches [...]. The Portuguese Cathedrals are *hallenkirchen*. They are covered by a single vaulting system, which is independent from the diverse configuration of the ribs in each bay. The vaults are supported by the outer walls and by pillars distributed through space. Goa's Cathedral vaulting is entirely different: the space of the three naves and transept is clearly discontinuous, its units are separated by singular vaults that only meet at the cross giving birth to a groin vault. [Apart from the fact that space has a clear longitudinal direction] the classification of the Cathedral of Goa as a false basilica is justified by the fact that the minimal difference between the height of the central and the lateral naves does not allow for the existence of clerestory windows, an essential element of a basilica.

The Cathedral of Goa's internal and external architectural mouldings are, without exception, what we could term 'Roman', the word used in Portugal and Spain throughout the 16th century to define the Renaissance Italianate type of design, whereas the Portuguese Cathedrals display several types of articulations, some 'Roman', others Modern (i.e., Gothic). With Nunes Pereira, I conclude from the essential differences in spatial arrangement, vaulting system and moulding design between the Cathedral of Goa and the other Portuguese Cathedrals of the second half of the 16th century, that the plan and the essential type of Goa was probably defined in Lisbon in the early 1560s and sent to Goa to be built here by local architects: a three-nave church with lateral inter-communicating chapels like the Cathedral of Portalegre, with a transept and a very deep chancel like Leiria, in order to accommodate a large canon's chapter in festive days. However, differing from my colleague, I would suggest that the original idea was not followed through.

Originally the type chosen probably included groin vaults supported by square pillars, the three naves being of equal or almost equal height and the vaults, like in Portugal, independent from the pillars, thus allowing for a continuous space to flow inside the church. The original proposal, in one word, was for a *hallenkirche*.

Cathedral, Old Goa, south tower

But this was not to be and for one simple reason: because the works were interrupted for 30 years. When Júlio Simão was charged with the continuation of the building in 1597, not only had times changed, but also Simão was not an architect of Portuguese training or culture. In fact, he was probably not Portuguese. Vítor Serrão has recently suggested that Simão was Italian, based on the fact that in the documents that he unearthed from Goa's archives, the architect is sometimes named Simonis. Other documents also revealed by him spell the name as Simões, which resembles Simonis. French or Spanish origins were already suggested by some writers in the past but these nationalities would correspond to names like Simon or Simón, not Simonis or Simões. But neither is Italian a good suggestion: the name would in this case be Simone. Therefore, I propose yet another possibility: maybe Simonis / Simões / Simão was the rendering in Portuguese of a name from a non-Latin-based language: Flemish, German or English. That was the habit of the times in Spain and Portugal: to 'transliterate' names that the Portuguese found difficult to pronounce. Be as it may, all the works attributed to Júlio Simão are different from anything built in Portugal at the time or even subsequently.

He must have received some Italian training. Italian architecture—and even Roman architecture at the closing decades of the 16th century—is where one finds the style that most

Cathedral, Old Goa, detail of the central nave

closely resembles what we see in some parts of the Cathedral of Goa: see the upper storeys of the surviving southern tower in the western façade (the northern one, which was certainly exactly alike, collapsed in 1776) or the quiet, correct and carefully arranged classical vocabulary and proportioning of the Cathedral's internal and external elevations. This is all typical of Italian Counter-Reformation architecture. It reminds me of many-a-wall articulation by Vasari or Giacomo della Porta.

Of course, there is nothing in the Sé of the refined Michelangelesque ornament or ambiguous articulations we find in Italy. But Júlio Simão must have immediately understood that he had to work with serious financial constraints, in an enormous building, very large even by Italian standards, and in the absence of skilled sculptors. The harmonious result of Simão's adaptation to circumstances is admirable. Also striking are the Flemish-like ornament of the main façade's doors. Flanders, and Flemish ornament as rendered by authors of architectural treatises, were a powerful cultural current in European architecture of the second half of the 16th century, as powerful as Italian influence.

In all of these aspects and many others, Júlio Simão's work in Goa closely reminds me of the career of Filippo Terzi (or Tércio) in Portugal. Terzio (1520–97) was an Italian architect and

Cathedral, Old Goa, detail of main door

military engineer who became instrumental in the changing of Portuguese architecture. He too designed quite unexpected buildings where Italian, Portuguese and Flemish architectural cultures blend. Terzi came to Portugal in 1578 in the cadre of a true 'invasion' of Portuguese military architecture and engineering by Italian professionals, which took place from the 1570s onwards spreading through Portuguese-controlled territories in Europe, the Atlantic, Brazil, Africa and Asia.

Apart from being an architect, Simão was also a military engineer. He worked actively in the fortifications of Goa. He was responsible for the design of Fort Aguada, to name but one well-known fortification, but he also made plans for Cochin, Daman, Bassein, Meliapor and many more sites. He was knighted in 1607 and was still designing and inspecting fortifications in Goa when he died around 1632.

It is my opinion that it was his choice to have the Cathedral vaulted with coffered barrel vaults supported by pillars that he made into a rectangular shape so they could take the arches that separate the naves. It was also he who conceived the pyramid-like buttressing system that discharges the weight of the central vault onto the lateral and of the lateral onto the

Cathedral, Old Goa, view of the north elevation

side chapels via buttresses between the aisle chapels. The southern lateral elevation of the Cathedral with the chapels placed between the buttresses is typical of Italian churches (to the north probably stood the space for the Cathedral's cloister, hence the incomplete elevation on that side).

Barrel vaults sometimes cause serious stability problems due to the pressure they put on walls, further intensified when low-density stone like Goan laterite is used and when the roofs, vaults and walls are subject to the torrential rains of the south-western monsoon. Everywhere in Goa we see buttresses stepping up against the lateral walls of vaulted chancels or naves in a not always successful attempt at keeping them from falling apart. Except at the Cathedral. The more monumental barrel vaults in Goa, those of the Cathedral, are the only ones that have not collapsed nor do they appear to be on the verge of collapse.

As he was beginning to work in the Cathedral and as the Arch of Vasco da Gama was being built, the commission for the design of the façade of the Jesuit's Bom Jesus church came into the order of the day. It is very likely that it was given to Júlio Simão.

The Façade of the Bom Jesus

In 1597, father Nicolau Pimenta, the Jesuit *Visitador* in India, i.e., the General's representative in this region, wrote a letter to the Society in Rome informing that a meeting had taken place at the college of São Paulo about the ongoing construction of the Jesuit's new building in Goa: the Professed House of the Bom Jesus. Works had reached its final stage one decade after building activity began in 1587. The *Casa Professa* was practically finished, including the church. Only its façade was yet to be built and that is precisely why the meeting was held: to reach a decision about the façade's design. As it is well know, in the said meeting the Jesuits decided to have the façade built with *pedra do norte*, northern stone, that is, Bassein granite, with the exception of the lateral orders, which would be in laterite like the walls to guarantee the correspondence between the façade's composition and the rest of building (in fact the existing façade presents itself as three vertical granite bands placed between the laterite pilasters that constitute its main architectural order).

Father Pimenta's letter gave notice of the façade's material but not of its design because the former was evidently to become much more expensive than the latter and that required the goodwill of the Society's headquarters. But the choice of both represented bold decisions by the Jesuits.

The building of the *Casa Professa* was from the start an ambitious but modest affair. There is no paradox in this. The ambition stood in the dimension of the complex which had been designed by the Italian *Visitador* Alessandro Valignano in the early months of 1586 with three

Church of the former Professed House of the Bom Jesus, façade, designed 1597

wings containing approximately 50 cells and many other rooms, distributed in three storeys around one large courtyard. Also ambitious was the chosen location, the important open space known as *Terreiro dos Galos*, just outside the old city wall, an option that was maintained against the opposition of the Franciscans, the *Misericórdia* and other city institutions who would rather not have the Jesuits so near the city centre. The *Casa Professa* was thus large and well located. But it was not monumental.

In the plans sent by Valignano to Rome there is room for the church but this is not represented. The caption of the drawing in Valignano's hand reads that the church could be either of three or of one nave. This means that, in 1586, the Jesuits had not yet decided whether they were going to remain faithful to the type tried out at S. Paulo or going for a single nave church. I would suggest that a debate around this issue was probably going on within the Society in Goa. The Jesuits in Rome or in Portugal had for long opted for single nave churches with lateral chapels as the appropriate type for the Society and the hesitation of Valignano could only be the result of the opinions of Goan priests used to the model of S. Paulo.

Whatever the case, the architect of the *Casa Professa*, who very likely was the Jesuit Domingos Fernandes (Dias 1999), designed a modest building undoubtedly in full agreement with his brethren: the church of the Bom Jesus is a single nave box without lateral chapels, covered by a roof (not a vault), an upper choir over the entrance, a deep box-like chancel with a coffered barrel-vault. At the origin it probably had a false transept.

Except in dimension, the church is the exact type of most of the parish churches in Goa. This could be because many were modelled on it but also because it took inspiration from some. Apparently the Jesuits had decided not to make too much of a spectacle out of their new architectural enterprise. But this attitude changed dramatically when the time came to build the façade in 1597.

The meeting at São Paulo presided over by the *Visitador* Nicolau Pimenta where it was decided that it would be built with *pedra do norte* was probably the occasion for a decisive shift from modesty to monumentality.

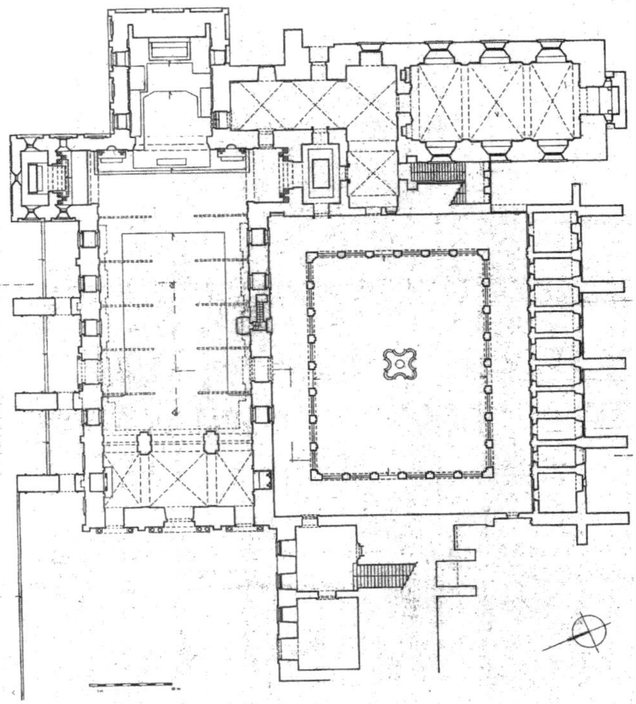

Professed House of the Bom Jesus, Old Goa, plan (Nunes Pereira, 2005)

I agree with Nunes Pereira's idea that the new façade was probably designed by Júlio Simão. The novelty of the ornamental articulation of the façade and of its architectural type is such that it was inconceivable that it was done by someone who already lived in Goa.

Simão had arrived from Europe the year before. We can imagine him with his mind full of ideas, sketch books displaying all his skills, collections of engravings and a couple of architectural treatises under his arm. He was already proving his capacity as a seductive designer of novel types of architectural ornament in the design for the Arch of Vasco da Gama and maybe even in the doorways for the Cathedral, also to be built in *pedra do norte*.

The Bom Jesus has a unique façade in the history of Christian architecture, one of the outstanding monuments of the architecture of India. Nunes Pereira (2005: 305 ff) discusses this façade at length, its careful inscription in a square up to the level of the main cornice, its highly unusual division in four orders. But my colleague's more engaging and provocative ideas concern the use of the orders and of ornament in the four storeys. According to him, Simão would have thought of a superposition of nations: the lower order, with its severe Serlian motives, represents Italy, the second, flowery and delicate, comprehends the ornaments used by Serlio in his French works and other buildings of this nation. The third order, with its very rare round windows and profuse Flemish ornament would stand for

Church of Bom Jesus, Old Goa, top orders of the façade

Flanders. The fourth and final order would represent the fusion of all nationalities in the architectural culture of Goa.

These are undoubtedly clever ideas but the building itself cannot vouch for them because stone is mute. Without text, letters, inscriptions, oral tradition, stone does not speak. Only we speak in its place, our speech relying upon the culture of our own times. For instance, I could show the first, second and fourth storeys of the façade as being as Flemish as the third based on my own interpretation of ornament and my reading of 16th-century architectural culture.

What seems to matter is the novelty and modernity of the Bom Jesus' church façade articulation. It must have had a profound impact on Goa's architectural culture: Flemish ornament, Serlian mouldings, round windows and French Serlian window frames, were subsequently used in simplified form throughout Goa in the 17th and early 18th centuries.

More immediately, the influence of the Bom Jesus can be seen, within Jesuit culture, in the Society's churches of Bassein (completed in 1636) and Diu (begun in 1601). Also, and more

Church of S. Paulo or Our Lady of Conception, Diu, begun 1601

importantly, it is probable that the Bom Jesus showed Indians that Catholic architecture could be as tactile in surface understanding, as minute in detail, as organic in form, as engaging for the eye, as the ornamental arts of the subcontinent. This was maybe the Bom Jesus' façade's more lasting contribution: it could have been the building that allowed Indian artisans to domesticate European architectural and ornamental vocabulary, to make it their own.

The Church of *Graça* at *Monte Santo*

A year before Viceroy Gama and the architect Júlio Simão, another decisive patron of the architecture and arts had arrived in Goa: Dom frei Aleixo de Menezes (1559–1617), Archbishop of Goa from 1595 to 1609, Governor of the *Estado*, 1607–09. He protected his own congregation, the Augustinians, by securing for them the complete renovation of the small convent they had built from 1572 at one of the more advantageous areas of Old Goa, the hill to the west of the city centre where the church of Rosário stood from the early 16th century. The hill soon witnessed so many religious constructions (the many Augustinian buildings, the Jesuits' new college of S. Roque, the convent of St. John of God) that it became known as *Monte Santo* (the Holy Mount).

Dom frei Aleixo arrived from Portugal with the design of a magnificent convent and church (dedicated to Nossa Senhora da Graça, Our Lady of Grace) to replace the Augustinians' old building. As per my reading of the relevant documents and chronicles discussed by Sidh Mendiratta (2003) and Vítor Serrão (2008), Dom frei Aleixo brought a plan, as was the habit of the times, which obviously implied a choice of *parti*, but no elevation drawings, no precise measurements, no situation of the building. These were left to local architects to work out. The documents make it quite clear, for instance, that the Augustinians had no preconceived idea about whether their church should be vaulted or covered by a simple roof.

Júlio Simão advised them to build a vault when he was consulted about the problem in 1608. He said that 'the church has sufficient foundations and walls to sustain a stone and brick vault' (Mendiratta: 14). This episode alone proves that he had not devised the general *parti* of the church but I think that Simão was then working closely with Manuel Coelho, the man who the documents identify as the church and convent's master mason, giving advice and drawings for several parts of the vast enterprise, among which, no doubt, were the vault of the church and its façade and towers.

The Augustinian convent occupied the crest of *Monte Santo* turned east towards downtown Goa. The church's towers became the city skyline's highest spires dominating the countryside for miles around as the ruin of its sole survivor still does. The church stood to the north of the large quadrangle of the convent, which was distributed around two cloisters with the chapter room in between them. The second cloister's wings, to the

Former church and convent of the Augustinians, Old Goa, view taken during the archaeological works in the year 2001 (photo S. Mendiratta)

south, passed above the road via an archway and were directly connected to another large complex of Augustinian buildings, the College of Nossa Senhora do Pópulo. The church's type, a single nave building with inter-communicating lateral chapels was perhaps new in Goa. But not in Portuguese India.

One of the strongest trends of European Catholic architecture in the 16th century was the unification and widening of the church's internal space in order to gather more people and to focus their attention on the Eucharist, in particular the cult of the Holy Sacrament, which was being renewed in the Christian world since at least the 15th century. This was obtained through the raising of all nave vaults to equal height or through the elimination of aisles in favour of inter-communicating lateral chapels, which allowed the service of private patrons and confraternities who patronized the side chapels without disturbing the services held in the central space.

Contrary to general belief, this antedates the Counter-reformation of the mid-16th century, at least in the Iberian Peninsula. The single nave with inter-communicating lateral chapels in a type of probable Catalan or Aragonese origin, which was introduced in Portugal in the 1480s and in Portuguese India, so far as I know, in the Dominican church of Chaul, Nossa Senhora de Gaudalupe (Our Lady of Guadalupe), begun in 1549, one year before the

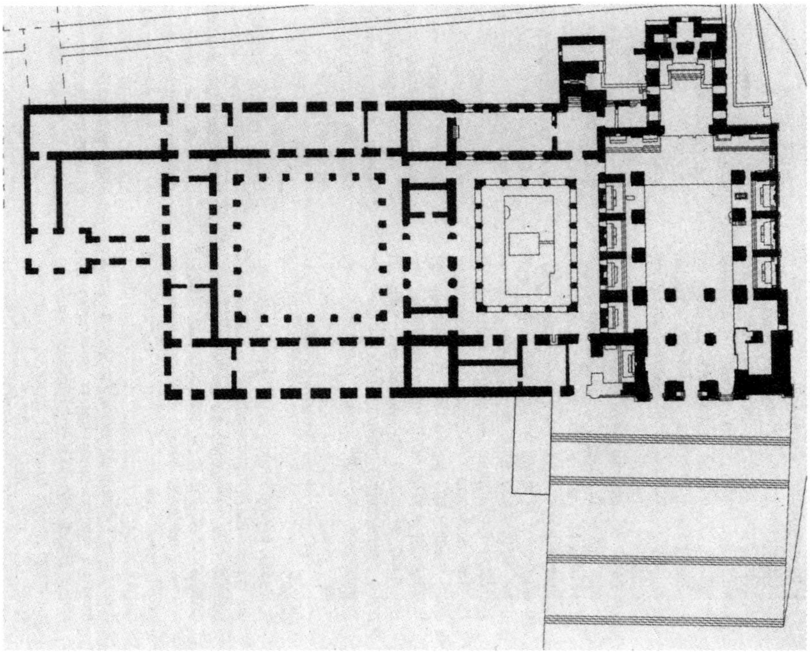

Plan by Sidh Mendiratta

Dominicans started building their convent in Goa. The church of Chaul, now a spectacular ruin used by local farmers as a shed, was very large (the nave was almost 30x15m) and one can still observe the gothic rib vaults of the inter-communicating chapels of its northern side. I often wonder whether the lateral chapels of the Dominican church in Goa that I have already discussed in this book (see Chaper 1) had passages between them. They probably did. The type also appears at the Franciscan church in Bassein, maybe at the main church of Chaul and, of course, at Goa's Cathedral.

But what we see in the plan of Nossa Senhora da Graça is the full maturity of the type as tried out in many Portuguese churches of the late 16th century, namely the Augustinian's mother church, S. Vicente de Fora in Lisbon, begun in 1582, and in hundreds of Italian and Spanish churches: a wide nave and lateral chapels as deep as half the nave's width, and an inscribed transept at which the lateral passages culminate. It is inevitable that one compares N. S. da Graça with Lisbon's S. Vicente de Fora: when Dom frei Aleixo sailed to Goa, S. Vicente was not only the Augustinian's more important church but also the more recent and a royal foundation by Philip I (Philip II of Spain).

Both churches are vaulted single-nave, inter-communicating lateral chapels, two-tower façade buildings. But they differ in the location of the friars' choir seats: whereas S. Vicente

N.S.da Graça, Old Goa, façade at the beginning of the 20th century (photo by Sousa & Paul)

S. Vicente de Fora, Lisboa, façade

has a retro-choir, i.e., a choir behind the main altar with the Holy Sacrament tabernacle placed in an arch between the nave and the choir, and a second choir over the entrance (which was probably built later), Graça had a choir in the chancel before the altar and a very large, very deep choir over the entrance, occupying both the space between the towers and the space over the first bay of the nave.

There is also another difference between the two churches: Graça had a *camarin* as demonstrated by Sidh Mendiratta. I shall return to this in the next chapter. Here it will suffice to mention that a *camarin* is a chamber where the tabernacle is placed, located high behind the main altar and open towards it. Before the congregation assembled in the church, the tabernacle appears bathed in the sunlight that illuminates the chamber from behind through windows opened in the church wall. In order for the *camarin* to work its wonders, the chancel cannot be too deep, otherwise the faithful in the nave wouldn't be able to see the altar properly. But the Goa Augustinians needed a very large choir and this is why Graça has such a very deep upper choir over the entrance.

The inter-communicating lateral chapels had no success in Goan architecture. I can only think of one or two churches that have adopted this type of plan in the 17th and 18th

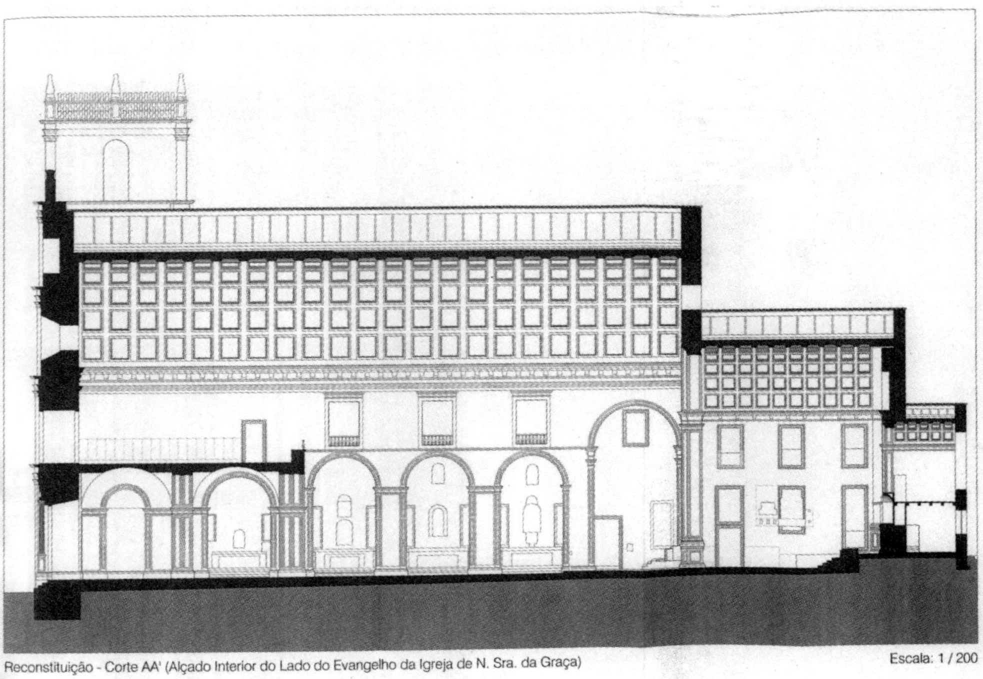

N.S. da Graça, Old Goa, longitudinal section (reconstitution), drawing by S. Mendiratta

centuries. This was probably due to the fact that private patrons, aristocratic or clerical, confraternities and other associations, never adopted or were allowed to adopt this type of chapel to locate their devotion.

The Augustinian church's more enduring contribution, indeed ground-breaking, for the architecture of Goa resided in its main façade: it was the first church in Goa with a two-tower façade, a type normally reserved for Cathedral churches that only the Sé had adopted. Subsequently, practically all parish and convent churches would have two towers.

The specific type of tower façade that one could see at Graça until the early 1930s (when it finally crumbled after a century of abandonment and the collapse of the church and convent) is unique and became one of the distinguishing traits of Goan architecture: nowhere else does one encounter façades organized in three superimposed orders plus a fourth order in the central bay, sided by five-order towers.

Church façades organized in more than three orders appear in central and northern Europe alone and even there they are not very common. I can only think of one reason why this type of façade would appear in Goa in the early years of the 17th century: its 'inventor' was a northern or central European architect of great creative capacity, probably Júlio Simão.

N.S. da Graça, Old Goa, façade, reconstitution, drawing by S. Mendiratta

Furthermore, the façade follows a local logic so to speak: the architect simply used the form of the façade of the Bom Jesus, which was recently completed, and placed towers at its flanks. With this façade, the Augustinian church managed to rival the Cathedral itself in prominence in Goa's skyline and in Goa's architectural imagination. Dom frei Aleixo was fully successful in boosting his order's importance in Goa.

Santa Mónica

Next to the friars' convent, Dom frei Aleixo and the Augustinians founded in 1606 and built between 1611 and 1627 the only full-fledged nunnery that existed until the 19th century in the Portuguese world from Africa to Macau: the convent of Santa Mónica with its church dedicated to Santa Maria.

This vast convent has survived practically intact the systematic and deliberate destruction of most of the convents of Goa perpetrated by Portuguese and Goan authorities and civil society during the 19th century. As was the case in European Portugal, the laws that extinguished the convents in the *Estado da Índia* after the 1840s in order to allow the new dominant class of landowners to appropriate their lands and other riches, exempted from this

Church and convent of Santa Mónica, Old Goa, 1611–1627, view from St. Augustine tower (photo S. Mendiratta)

fate the nunneries until the last nun died a natural death, in recognisance of the fact that nuns would have no way of fending for themselves outside the cloister. To this we owe the survival of many convents in Portugal and of Santa Mónica in Goa, because when the last nuns died in the late 19th century times had changed and the voracity of the convent vultures was contained by a more sensitive public opinion.

Santa Mónica is a typical Iberian convent, the likes of which can be found everywhere in Portugal, Spain and Latin America, a vast quadrangle with the church to one of its sides, located parallel to the street. A nunnery is the dwelling and worship place for women who are confined to its walls and courtyards. The precinct that separates a nunnery from the outside world cannot be entered by laymen. Even priests may only enter the cloister in special and controlled circumstances. The nunnery church is a particularly delicate place in the monastic complex because it must be used by two communities that cannot enter in close contact with each other: the nuns and the laity. They have to celebrate mass together but must stand apart. The nuns have to see the altar but they should not be seen by the laity. They have to confess and receive communion but the priest cannot enter the cloister. A sacristy is necessary but the celebrant should not access it through cloistered areas. Nuns have to contact their families, and even to entertain close relatives, they have to administer properties and participate in business meetings with their representatives but cannot even see, let alone touch them.

To respond to all of these programmatic requirements a type of monastic church appeared in the Middle Ages and was implemented, with various sub-types, throughout the Christian world. The church of Santa Mónica is a good example of the most common sub-type of the Iberian world. Or, rather, it was: with the dying of the nuns and the barring of new admissions (the last nun died in Santa Mónica in 1885), the convent entered a phase of rapid decadence: in 1849 the roof of the church's nave collapsed. Probably because of this, three huge buttressing arches were built to prevent the whole façade from crumbling (these arches, which render the place so conspicuously picturesque in spite of defacing the building, do not appear in the plans of Old Goa made in the 1780s and this is why I conclude that they were built later).

The conventual church like so many others, was divided into two separate churches designated by old texts as 'inside' and 'outside' churches (*de dentro* and *de fora*). The latter was the public church, open to the laity and the celebrants. The former was the nun's choir or choirs (for there were often many), accessible to the mothers only, from where they participated in the public celebrations and where they held the internal ceremonies of the convent.

As we can still see at Santa Mónica, these parts of the building are aligned alongside the street and the public entrance is lateral so that the laity, as they enter the public church and face the altar, turn their backs to the nun's choir, located to the end of the building opposing the altar. The nun's choir, or two superimposed choirs, were separated from the public church by grills, which were provided with heavy curtains and fierce iron spikes, which functioned more as rhetorical signs of enclosure than effective means of separation.

Santa Mónica church, however, displays a very unusual typological trait, at least in what concerns Portuguese nunnery churches: it has two public doors. We see three doors along the façade: two doors lead to the public church, the third, some distance away, is the convent's door that exists in every convent, giving access to the nun's *Portaria* and the *Locutório*, that is, the nunnery visiting room, where the two worlds used to meet separated by grills and curtains. To my knowledge there are only two other nunneries in the whole of the Portuguese world with a double door public church. They are both in south Portugal, near the Spanish border, they are both Franciscan and both were built at the same time as Santa Mónica: Santa Clara in Évora, and Servas in Borba.

Double door public churches exist in a handful of nunneries in central Spain and in central Mexico. I have often wondered about reasons for the double door and for their

Church of Santa Mónica, Old Goa, doors

rarity: separate entrances for men and women or for different classes of people? Why in some churches only, then? Why in so few regions? I have read many books and articles, posed questions to many colleagues, many priests, and to some nuns. I still have no answer. What the double doors prove, however, is the very strong Spanish influence exerted upon the people who programmed and built Santa Mónica and that is sufficiently significant for my purpose here.

Another important proof of that influence is the façade type. I have already called this type a pseudo-frontal façade (V. Gomes 2000). There are many in Spain and in Portugal but Santa Mónica was chronologically the first in the Portuguese world. These façades were designed as if they had behind them a church axially aligned and not, as is the case, extending longitudinally with its internal axis parallel to the façade.

Santa Mónica's public church façade is divided laterally into 5 bays. In the ground floor the two doors occupy bays 2 and 4. The central bay, bay 3, displays a large stone plaque with an inscription containing the fundamental data about the convent's foundation. Above the cornice, this bay is also given axis prominence by a central tabernacle-like motif (with a niche with the image of Santa Mónica) connected to the bays on its sides by scrolls, precisely

Church of Santa Mónica, Old Goa, façade

like a regular façade for a 'normal' church. When one looks at Santa Mónica from the outside, the presence of the nun's church (the choir), is made very discrete and only the public church stands to attention as if all other constituent parts of the convent were meant to disappear from public view. This was the main objective of pseudo-frontal façades in nunnery churches: to disguise the presence of a peculiar type of church, a 'subordinate' type of church, by presenting it as a 'normal' church.

Capela do Monte

The elegance of the articulation of Santa Mónica's public church façade is similar to the elevation solutions we find at the Capela de Nossa Senhora do Monte (Our Lady of the Mount), a parish church built on top of the easternmost hill of Old Goa at the end of the 16th or the beginning of the 17th century replacing a previous chapel erected there since the early years of the Portuguese conquest.

The chapel of Our Lady of the Mount is in fact not a chapel, at least not in European terms. It is a large single nave church covered with a coffered barrel vault. The chancel is lower than the nave but quite deep and has the same kind of vault. The vocabulary of the

N.S. do Monte, Old Goa, last years of the 16th century/early years of the 17th century

N.S. do Monte, interior, view from the upper choir

building's external façades and of its vaults is quite elaborate. The vault and the internal lateral walls are divided into three bays. The exterior southern elevation facing the main approach to the church is also divided into three bays corresponding to the interior division. The central bays of the vault and internal wall are different from the lateral ones. Each vault's bay consists of five rows of coffers but the central row in the central bay is wider than the others as it corresponds to the single window placed above the lateral door. The lateral bays both display two narrow windows at the upper tier. At the lower one, the eastern bay has one window only, in contrast with the western bay, which displays two windows larger than all the others.

The external south façade is, therefore, not precisely symmetrical but it is obvious that it behaves like a frontal façade with a clear-cut symmetry axis. This is due to the fact that, in many ways, it really was the church's main façade. In fact, it stands at the top of a very wide and simple 50 steps-staircase cut out of the hill's slope, which was certainly used when large crowds visited the church and even for open-air masses. The frontal façade, on the other hand, faces west, thus being located too close to the hill's ravine edge. There was room enough to build the traditional cross there but the area was too narrow to welcome the crowds visiting the pilgrimage church that Our Lady of the Mount obviously became. Approached primarily from the south, the church was built with that location in mind: the façade is very elegant, more becoming a noble house than a modest church. As time passed, the attendance at the church diminished substantially and the monsoon rains heavily hit the south door. It was condemned in the late 18th century.

Styles

The Cathedral, Nossa Senhora da Graça, Santa Mónica, Monte, seem to have created two complementary but different styles for the design of elevations, doors and windows of the churches of Goa, both of which are extraordinarily refined and elegant.

The first style is Flemish. *Pedra preta* or *pedra do norte* was often used for the carving of main doors and window mouldings in this style. *Pedra do norte* was the dark granite and basalt

Bom Jesus, Old Goa, lateral door to the church

from the *Província do Norte*'s quarries near Bassein, namely Dongri, located on the south bank of the river facing the northern capital. The mouldings of this style are of the same type at the Cathedral, the Bom Jesus, S. Mónica and N.S. da Graça. Portuguese architectural historians know these mouldings very well. They were common throughout Portugal in the same period due to the influence of the treaty of Serlio, the ephemeral architecture of arches and funeral or triumphal monuments and many engravings of Flemish or German provenance: the motives were known in the Northern countries as *strapwerk* (leather work-inspired motives), *rollwerk* (lace work), and *ferronerie* (metal work). They formed cartouches, door, window or coffer frames, corbels, metopae, etc. The main doors of the Cathedral, the church and convent doors of Santa Mónica, the doors and windows of the Bom Jesus, all show this international Flemish decoration at its best in Goa. Only the hard northern stone could do justice to the refinement of the carving because it didn't lose shape with successive layers of whitewashing.

Salvador do Mundo, Loutolim, founded 1581, rear façade

However, a second style, made of simpler architectural mouldings of a sober classical Italian inspiration, could be sculpted in Goan laterite and then covered in plaster and whitewashed without loosing definition. This was the preferred treatment for secondary windows and doors and especially for whole wall surfaces, exterior and interior, frontal or lateral. Complete or incomplete pilastered orders, architraves, friezes and cornices, simple geometrical divisions of walls, all finely designed and executed, all resplendent in their whiteness, give Goan façades a prominence which is very different from anything seen in Portugal aside from frontal façades. In fact, Portuguese churches have all ornamental or architectural richness concentrated on the frontal façade. Not so in Goa. Depending on the location of the church building, at least one lateral façade (the best examples being Monte at Old Goa and the church of Rachol), and very often even the rear façade of the main-chapel (see the church of Salvador do Mundo – Saviour of the World – at Loutolim, for instance), are treated, with great simplicity and elegance, as worthy architectural compositions. If there is a 'purist' classicism anywhere outside Europe it is this.

Take a remarkable Goan church façade that was probably designed by the same architect who was in charge of Our Lady of the Mount: that of the church of Carambolim, to the

S. João Baptista, Carambolim, façade, late 16th or early 17th century

N.S. do Monte, Old Goa, façade

east of Old Goa. Carambolim was one of the more important rural parishes around the old capital and it played a crucial role in the 'black legend' of its downfall: it would have been the poisoning of the waters of the then famous lake of Carambolim, which served many important paddy fields, that triggered the diseases that led to the progressive abandonment of the capital. Furthermore, Carambolim was, with Divar, the stage of the first mass conversions to Christianity in Goa and it was at this church that, for the first time a Goan priest, André Vas, celebrated mass in 1558 (Mascarenhas 2009: 119 for bibliography).

The church, founded before 1553, is a single nave building covered by a roof. The chancel, covered by a barrel vault, is located to the south, the façade is turned north towards the road from Old Goa. It faces a very large *terreiro* where the festivity of St. John the Baptist took place with the presence of the Viceroy and all the nobility from Goa. The church now has a bell tower on its eastern flank. It was added in the mid-19th century and I am convinced that the slightly withdrawn one-storey-high lateral bays, one of which supports the tower, are also late additions.

Carambolim's façade is a variation upon Our Lady of the Mount's. It is three-bay wide, three-order high in the central bay, the door is framed by exempt columns, all orders are articulated by pilasters shafts inscribed with frames. The lower order is almost a direct copy of the Mount's, the upper stories simplifying the prototype by eliminating pediments. However, an attic is added to its cornice thus making the façade higher and more like the vertical rectangle of the Bom Jesus.

The overall composition of both façades (that are visible from each other above coconut groves and hills) is derived almost directly from architectural treatises like Serlio and the Flemish Vredeman De Vries (1565): see the very elegant top sections with central oculi within squares. These forms also appear in the crowning of Velha Goa's Cathedrals transept arms and in the church of Carmoná, dated 1606, here with Flemish-type decoration around the oculus. These top sections are so Flemish in appearance that they constantly remind me of the many-peaked gabled façades of Flemish houses in Brussels, Antwerp, Mâlines or Gand.

The architect of Monte and Carambolim was probably the same as that of the Cathedral, of the Bom Jesus façade, of Santa Mónica, of the Augustinian's façade, of many other churches throughout Goa (Loutolim, the Seminary church at Rachol, etc.). He was a master of both Flemish form and ornament, and of classicist purism.

The Missing Carmel

It is a great shame for Goa and a great pity for its architectural history that the church and convent of the Carmelites had totally disappeared in the 20th century. It was a singular building in the context of the Old City. What we know about the form of the convent, founded in 1612 and completed in 1634 by the Discalced Carmelites, a Spanish order with Spanish and Italian religious and artistic culture, shows that at least the church was an Italian building, the first purely Italian building in Goa (but not the last as we shall see).

Commenting upon its lone façade, when nothing else of the whole complex remained, father Gabriel de Saldanha wrote, in the second volume of his *História de Goa política e arqueológica* (1926), that it was of "little aesthetical value". For our eyes and culture, for modern architectural history, the Carmelite façade was the most strikingly splendid Roman-type façade Goa has ever had. But, of course, this is probably why good father Gabriel didn't like it: he was a partisan of neo-gothic values and an active opponent of the Renaissance. Furthermore, it was convenient for him and others to dislike the Carmelite ruin: after all, the demolition of Old Goa's buildings was the enterprise at which a certain Goan elite had given the best of its time for a century.

Church of the Carmelites, Old Goa, remains of the façade in the early 20th century (photo Sousa & Paul)

The information available about the church are the mass-plan of the convent in the Pombaline plans of Old Goa of the late 18th century, a distorted printing of a drawing commissioned by Lopes Mendes and three photographs by Sousa & Paul: a frontal and a retro-view of the façade and a view of the door.

From these we conclude that the church had a single nave with three lateral chapels per side. The nave was probably covered by a vault, the type of which is unknown to us. The chancel also had lateral chapels, four per side. We can see in the drawing published in Lopes Mendes' book that it was covered with what probably was a barrel vault with penetrations. I am convinced that all of these lateral chapels were connected by passages like in the Augustinian church or the Cathedral because that was the common Italian solution at the time. There was an upper choir over the entrance. A contemporary source quoted by padre Saldanha praises the decoration of the vault (we don't know whether this refers to the nave or the chancel) with its "exquisite and capricious relief", a probable reference to stucco ornament, maybe of the Flemish type.

The plan of Old Goa shows that the church was located, with the convent behind it, atop a wide staircase that led to a vast *terreiro* in front of the façade. The Discalced Carmelites

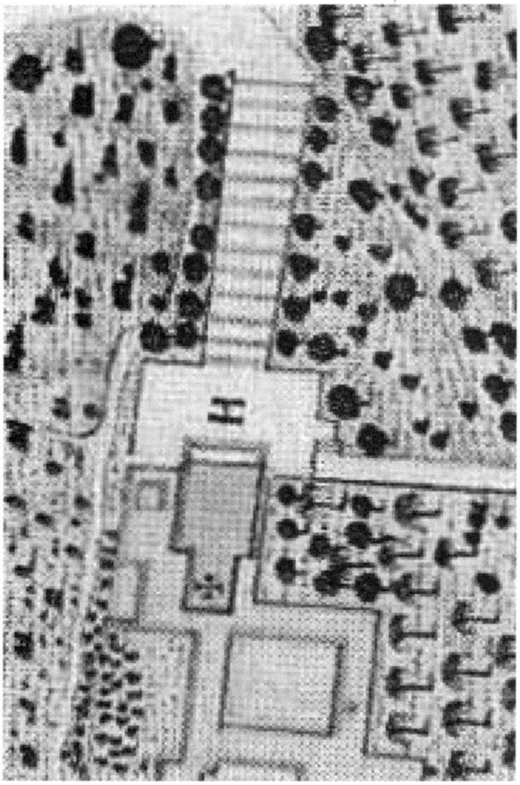

Plan of the Carmelite convent, detail of the plan of Old Goa by José de Morais Antas Machado (Direccção dos Serviços de Engenharia, Estado-Maior do Exército, Lisbon)

Lopes Mendes, ruins of the Carmelite church, Old Goa

were famous for the *Sacromonti*, the Sacred Hills representing the location of the martyrdom of Christ in Jerusalem, that they built in their convents throughout the world in order to reaffirm their belief of being the earliest of all Christian monastic orders and their link with the land of Palestine (V. Gomes 2005). I propose that the staircase shown in the plan had little chapels or altars on each of its steps. According to the plan these steps numbered 12 and I suppose this is accurate. The *terreiro* would have had the 13th chapel. Inside the church would have stood the 14th, the last Step of Christ's Passion.

Central Plan Chapels

Churches or chapels designed to a centralized plan, be it circular, a regular polygon or a cross with equal arms (a greek cross), were one of the more inventive and fruitful currents of Christian architecture from the Middle Ages to the Modern Era and from the eastern Mediterranean regions to northwestern Europe. The centralized plan was never chosen at random or for purely formal reasons. The vast majority of churches of this type are dedicated to the Virgin Mary. From ancient times, the circle and figures derived from the circle were considered symbols of Our Lady. The type was also adopted in many churches dedicated to the Holy Sacrament, to the Passion of Christ or to martyred Saints. This was because the Eucharist is an invocation of the body and blood of Christ, the first martyr, and therefore of His sepulchre, and the Holy Sepulchre basilica in Jerusalem was perceived as having been a centrally planned building (this is also why the Eucharist tabernacles are always centrally planned micro-architectures); and also because the Roman church of Santa Maria of all the Martyrs was installed in a round building, the ancient Roman Pantheon.

Saints who lived their lives as hermits in isolated places were worshipped in central plan buildings because these were conceived as representations both of the caves or huts in which the Saints would have lived and of the *martyrium* to which they dedicated their lives. Saints to the cult of whom pilgrimages were dedicated also had centrally planned votive chapels, these being the focal point of large gatherings on festive occasions. These chapels were usually built on the outskirts of important towns.

Very few churches or chapels of this type were built in Portuguese India. The most important of them all was the Theatine's Nossa Senhora da Divina Providência in Old Goa (Our Lady of the Divine Providence), begun in 1656, also known as S. Caetano, to which I will make ample reference later in this book, an outstanding building in the European architectural tradition. Its plan, a greek cross inscribed in a square, while characteristic of the Theatine's tradition also descends from a very old tradition of eastern Mediterranean origin.

The other cases of central plan buildings are little chapels, the majority of which have not survived intact until the present day. The first were built in or around Old Goa in the mid-16th century and therefore bear testimony to the European classical culture of the city's elite at the time. To track the remains of these chapels or of their memory in Goa, I shall resort to late 16th- and early 17th-century cartography: the view of Old Goa by the Dutch Jan Huygen Van Linschoten, dated 1595, and the drawings of Goa's territory by Pedro Barreto de Resende in António Bocarro's report of circa 1635.

These drawings are not exact but they are true: no geographical or architectural notation in them is gratuitous or invented: every bay, every hill, every group of houses, church, convent, tower, existed at the time the drawings were made. Linschoten's drawing is a view, not a map in any contemporary sense of the word. Barreto de Resende's image is more of an inventory of fortresses, religious settlements and villages existing at the time the report was completed. But we can trust both, not for the precision of forms but for approximate location and architectural type.

Linschoten represents the islands of Tiswadi (or Goa), Santo Estevão (now Combarjuá), *Ilha Nova* (now Juá), Divar, Chorão, and a sketchy view of the periphery of the surrounding territories. Central plan churches were a prestigious type of building at the time he was in India and went back to the Low Countries and had his drawings engraved. Therefore he took careful note of the difference between 'normal' and central plan buildings. The drawing shows three of these: Santo Amaro, that he places to the south of Our Lady of the Mount in Old Goa,

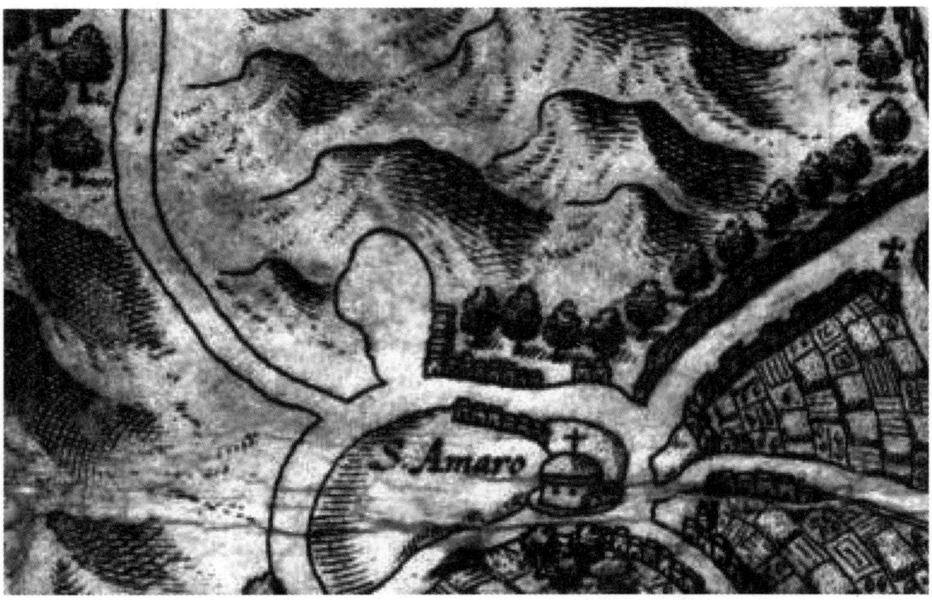

Chuch of Santo Amaro, Old Goa, detail of Linschoten's plan of 1595

Santo António (Saint Anthony), still existing at *Monte Santo*, and Santo André (St. Andrew), represented as a square building and located to the southwestern outskirts of Old Goa.

The most interesting of the three is Santo Amaro. Linschoten's drawing shows what appears to be a quite large round building with a small exo-narthex. It so happens that in 1549 a chapel of Santo Amaro was built in the western outskirts of Lisbon to a central plan design by an unknown architect, which stands out in European architecture for its originality derived from a Serlian prototype: it consists of two little cylinders of different dimension (the nave and the chancel), covered by semi-hemispherical vaults, to which a seven-bay portico is attached.

The cult of Santo Amaro appeared in the Iberian Peninsula in the Middle Ages. He was the patron Saint of people who undertook long and perilous sea travel as the Saint

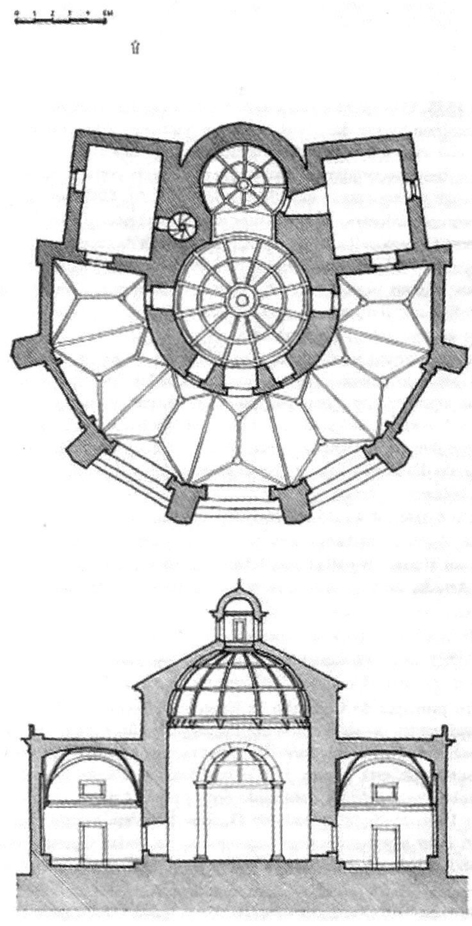

Santo Amaro, Lisboa, plan (Kubler, 1972)

Santo Amaro in Pedro Barreto de Resende's map of Old Goa, ca. 1635

himself is said to have done across the Atlantic in search of mythical paradisiacal islands, a typical Mediaeval narrative. Therefore Saint Amaro was a singularly appropriate figure to be worshipped in Portugal and in Goa in the 16th century.

The Goan chapel, built upon a hillock in the outskirts of the city like the one in Lisbon, was still in existence in 1635 when Pedro Barreto de Resende did his drawing but, by then, the rectangular exo-narthex or portico seems to have grown in size becoming a church nave and even sporting a tower.

No reference is made to Santo Amaro by the 19th- and 20th-century writers and no images have survived. The 1910 map of the archaeological commission (the map of Old Goa upon which all modern maps are based) shows the *lugar*, the location, of the chapel, thus indicating that it had disappeared. The same story can be told of Santo André, another central plan chapel, now square, shown by Linschoten. It was still standing in 1635, it was ignored by Cottineau de Klogen, Lopes Mendes, Nicolau da Fonseca, Gabriel de Saldanha and only its location is indicated in the 1910 map.

Saint Andrew, an Apostle of Christ, was a disciple of John the Baptist and a martyr, and this alone would justify the central plan of the chapel, which, although small, could have been designed to have an X-shaped organization of the internal space like most churches dedicated to Saint Andrew who was crucified in a cross of this type.

Santo António is the only still standing church indicated as having a central plan by Linschoten. The drawing shows a perfectly round structure with a square exo-narthex or chancel to the east. As it stands, Santo António is the strangest church in Old Goa, not

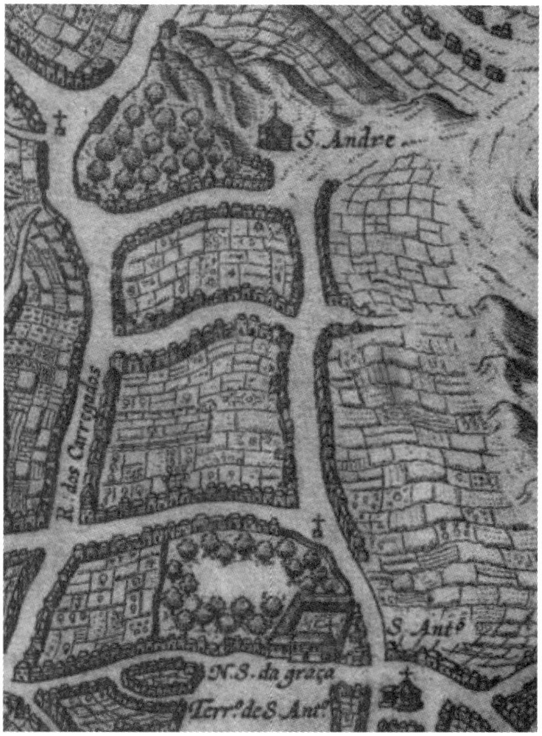

Santo André (to the south – top of the drawing) and Santo António (to the north – bottom of the drawing) in Linschoten panorama

because of its type, which is absolutely normal: a single nave covered by a roof and a lower chancel with a penetrations vault that I will discuss in a subsequent chapter, but on account of its convex façade (an half-circle in plan) that shelters an internal three-arch narthex under un upper choir covered by a hemispherical vault.

I believe that this strange façade is what remains of the original round chapel. The drawing by Pedro Barreto de Resende shows that the church had already been transformed in 1635 into a longitudinal building: we see that a door towards the east was already opened in the rotunda, that a nave was added, with a lateral door, and that a structure that was probably a chancel topped by a tower stood to the east. This chancel was replaced in the late 17th century by the beautiful vaulted main-chapel that we see today.

One of Barreto de Resende's drawing shows two other central plan chapels. They still exist. They are *ermidas* rather than chapels: Nossa Senhora da Nazaré (Our Lady of Nazareth) at Siridão, a building that suffered many transformations and is the object of veneration and frequent use, and, quite prominently, S. Jerónimo (St. Jerome) on the island of Chorão, a completely forgotten little building recently rediscovered. Both chapels were founded in the 16th century.

Santo António, Old Goa,
16th and 17th centuries, façade

Seminary of Chorão (destroyed), engraving pub. by Lopes Mendes 1886, distortion digitally corrected

A drawing in Lopes Mendes's book, distortedly printed as usual, shows the Jesuit seminary of Chorão as it still stood in the mid 19th century. It is one of the more impressive illustrations in the book. One looks and wonders: here is one of the largest built complexes created by Europeans in Early Modern Asia, one of the more elaborate architectural masterpieces of Goa and it has vanished practically to the last stone. In fact, the Seminary was systematically dismounted since it was shut down in 1859 by order of Governor Count of Torres Novas after a 50-year long campaign of discredit based on the narrative that it would be impossible to live in Chorão on account of terrible sanitary and health conditions.

There, in Chorão, all we now see is a quiet, we could almost say, innocent hillock. Looking carefully among vegetation and scattered stones, steps leading to one of the Mandovi's backwater margins can be traced on its northern slope. But the only built memory of the once proud Seminary of Chorão is the chapel of St. Jerome that crowns the hill. Since it was restored, the chapel can now be seen from as far as Panjim, shining white against its green backdrop. Lopes Mendes had it enhanced completely out of scale in his drawing and now it is completely out of context.

However, I suspect that the chapel was there before the Seminary, when in 1558 the Jesuit bishop João Nunes Barreto established his *quinta* (farm) on the site that later gave birth to the Seminary. The dedication of chapels in palatial gardens to St. Jerome, a hermit Saint and a scholar (he was one of the Doctors of the church), was traditional among Portuguese aristocrats.

What we see now, after the recent reintegration works, is a small cylinder covered by a roof with a blind lantern, surrounded by a polygonal eight-pillar portico supporting a

Location of the Seminary of Chorão and chapel of S. Jerónimo (built 1558)

Chapel of S. Jerónimo, Chorão, partial view

roof all around the rotunda. But this is neither what is shown by Lopes Mendes nor what Cottineau de Klogen described: images and text speak of columns, not pillars. The rotunda was surrounded by a colonnade. I don't know whether the columns were stolen as was everything else in the Seminary or are 'entombed' inside the pillars.

De Klogen lived in the age of neoclassicism. He therefore saw a *tholos* on Chorão's hill:

'A small chapel with an elegant dome, and Grecian pillars supporting the edifice; giving the whole from a distance the true appearance of a scenery from Greece.'

Grecian pillars, in the parlance of those times, were Doric columns, those that we see in Lopes Mendes (the vision of a "scenery from Greece", of course, was also induced by the fact that the Seminary was a school, an Academy of sorts). A century later, in 1927, Gabriel de Saldanha paraphrased Klogen referring to the same "Greek style pillars" and informed us that the chapel had been restored by private initiative in 1901.

The other still existing 16th-century round chapel, Our Lady of Nazareth, now wrongly identified with Jesus of Nazareth, stands at the top of a promontory over the mouth of the

N.S. da Nazaré (also known as Jesus Nazareth)

N.S.da Nazaré in Pedro Barrete de Resende's panorama, ca. 1635

Zuari river in the south coast of Tiswadi. Pedro Barreto de Resende made it as large as the more important churches outside of Old Goa, as large as his drawing of the chapel of Chorão (he obviously liked centrally planned buildings). The drawing shows what appears to be a building composed of two roofed rotundas. Today there is a large rotunda covered with a dome, which is the result of works carried out in 1906 (*Memória* 1933: 266) to which a nave and a frontal façade were added in recent times. The early 20th-century-modified rotunda presents a much too low profile, its windows and doors are modern, its dome recent.

There is another round chapel dedicated to Our Lady that could have been founded in the mid-sixteenth century: it still exists and it is the most handsome of all little central plan buildings in Goa. Its location is Naroá, on the island of Divar (Cipriano C. Gomes 1902).

It is a large chapel, round, articulated by pilasters and covered by a semi-hemispherical dome with a lantern at its crowning. Balustrades run around the main cornice and the lantern. Sphere-bearing pinnacles top the side pilasters of the rotunda. An ugly shed-like longitudinal nave was recently added to its eastern side.

N.S. da Candelária, Naroá, Divar, founded 1543, rebuilt 1633 and redecorated 1763

The chapel is today known as Nossa Senhora da Candelária (Our Lady of Candlemas) but I believe it received this dedication when it was subjected to an extensive redecoration in 1763 under the initiative of Viceroy Manuel de Saldanha (his intervention shows in the typically mid-18th century round windows and oculi with counter-curve pediments that adorn the rotunda). Our Lady of Candlemas (or Purification) is a devotion characteristic of fishermen, which became quite common in the Iberian Peninsula in the 18th century. It appears that a similar devotion emerged among the same community in Goa. Fr. Nascimento Mascarenhas recently told the story of the fisherfolk of Baina, Mormugão, who approached Archbishop Santa Catarina in 1796 for permission to have a chapel of their own, which would be autonomous from the church of Santo André. This chapel was dedicated to N.S. da Candelária (Mascarenhas 2006: 122).

The original chapel in Divar was founded in 1543. A century later, in 1633, it must have been extensively rebuilt. The date appears at the base of the image of Our Lady; and the door to the rotunda is a characteristic Renaissance doorway; two thin pilasters support a steep triangular pediment with no frieze in between them.

N.S. da Candelária, Naroá, Divar, original doorway and interior

N.S. da Candelária, Pilerne, 1779

N.S. da Candelária, Pilerne
(defaced in the late 20th century)

The devotion of 18th-century Portuguese patrons to N.S da Candelária, perhaps responding to local initiative, was confirmed in 1779 by the construction of a chapel of that invocation at Pilerne by Archbishop Assunção e Brito (1773–80) who, as we shall see later, was responsible for some important up-to-date architectural interventions in several churches in Goa. The chapel probably was rebuilt in its original form in 1888 (*Memória* 1933: 262).

The chapel at Pilerne stands atop a slope turned towards the northwest and it is visible from afar. It is an octagonal building with a salient chancel to the side opposite the entrance—a type of plan unique in Goa but very common in Portugal. Like a pilgrimage chapel that it was (and still is), a long staircase leads to it. An older staircase, with capriciously curved baroque steps, is partially visible approaching the chapel's *terreiro* from the west. Its architectural type, its location and its visibility give it the appearance of a North Portugal Marian shrine. In recent days the chapel was virtually destroyed by a huge (and extremely ugly) portico.

There are probably more round, square or polygonal chapels throughout Goa, some unknown to me, others transformed in recent times. It would be interesting to establish a

N.S. dos Remédios, Monte Cuelim, Cansaulim, uncertain original dates, probably early 17th century

complete inventory. The chapel of Our Lady of Remedies at Monte Cuelim, Cansaulim, is an interesting case. It stands atop a hill from where one enjoys the most magnificent view of the coast of Salcete from the Mormugão plateau to the Cabo de Rama. Looking at the building from outside it seems like a late-18th century longitudinal chapel until we notice that the part corresponding to the chancel is higher than the nave, which is quite unusual. Once inside we immediately understand why: the nave is a later addition to an original square chapel covered by a groin vault, very likely built in the second half of the 17th century.

3

The Origin of Goan Church Architecture in the Second Half of the 17th Century

Turning Point: The Decade of 1650

During the decade of 1650 the city of Old Goa underwent an architectural change as profound as half a century before in the generation of Julio Simão. This time, however, the change did not come about because of Viceregal initiative but from within the religious orders which, in emulation of wealth and power, decided to renovate their convents and houses in the city. This cycle began with two buildings: the new sacristy and ante-sacristy at the Jesuit's Bom Jesus, begun in 1652, and the church of the Theatines begun in 1655. The most significant contribution of these buildings to the formation of a characteristic Goan architecture was their exuberant use of the barrel vault with lateral penetrations and of the planed groin vault. Until then, as we know, the designers of churches used barrel vaults and in the previous chapter I have already pointed to the stability problems created by this type of vault during the Indian monsoon and with laterite stone construction.

The barrel vault with lateral penetrations and the planed groin vault are two different types of vault, the latter of Gothic origin. These new types are lighter than the barrel vault because they exert a more horizontal thrust and their weight is distributed through selected points of pressure rather than in a uniform way along the wall. These vaults have the additional advantage of permitting the opening of windows above the cornice to allow hot air to escape. Architects working under Goan light immediately realized that they could create interiors of extraordinary luminosity and decorate their vaults with stucco coffers or patterns with imaginative forms and colours that would shine under the razing light coming from the windows. The Goan church interior was thus created.

It is difficult for us to appreciate how novel the 1650s vaults might have appeared to

Lateral vault of N.S. da Divina Providência, Old Goa, after 1656

Goan observers. Most of the Cathedral's lateral chapels and its under-choir had planed groin vaults, which would have been completed by 1630. But these were probably perceived as secondary vaulting systems compared to the splendid barrel vaults of the lofty central naves. We also already know that the church of the Carmelites built between 1612 and 1634 had one or more barrel vaults with lateral penetrations decorated in a fashion that attracted much attention.

Both the barrel vault with lateral penetrations and the planed groin vault are uncommon in Portuguese architecture of the 16th and 17th centuries, although they appear frequently in the Gothic period. This is yet another case that demonstrates that Goan architecture is as close to European non-Portuguese architecture as it is to Portuguese. The first groin vaults between arches similar to those we see in Goa appear in Portugal in the church of the convent of Mafra after the 1720s under direct Italian influence. In fact, these vaults with penetrations are so rare in Portugal that architectural historians have not paid any attention to early modern types of vaulting in Portuguese architecture. Only a handful of cases come to my mind, all dated from the second half of the 17th century and those are much less spectacular than the Goan. The fact that these Portuguese vaults were to be painted and that

Cathedral, Old Goa, vault under the upper-choir

the paintings have often disappeared contributes to their banal appearance compared to the Goan and it also explains why very little attention has been paid to them historically.

I would tentatively point towards what is now Belgium (and was in the 17th century the Spanish Low Countries) for a possible origin of the Goan groin and barrel vaults with lateral penetrations raised after the 1650s. One should bear in mind that some of the more important Jesuit churches in Europe were built in this region precisely after the 1620s including what was possibly the first church in the world dedicated to St. Francis Xavier, the Jesuit church of Bruges (begun 1619). Almost all of these Belgian Jesuit churches were three-nave churches with groin or barrel vaults supported by columns, the church of Antwerp begun in 1615 being the remarkable exception with its simple barrel vault (De Jonge and Ottenheym 2007). The vaults themselves are sometimes quite similar to Goan examples: the vaults of Margão and Talaulim, which I will examine below, are of the same type as the ones of the Jesuit church of Namur (begun 1621), and the vaults of Divar equal those of Bruges or Louvain (begun 1650). Jesuit vaults in Belgium are often classical renderings of the Gothic groin vaults, which one can see in churches and cathedrals throughout the Low Countries, and in North-western and Central Europe in general.

Jesuit church of Namur, Belgium, beg. 1621

Jesuit church of Bruges, Belgium, beg. 1650, vault

Jesuit church of Louvain (Leuven), Belgium, beg. 1650, vault

Perhaps the German Jesuit churches, in particular those of South Germany built in the early years of the 17th century (Smith 2002), should also be mentioned in this context, not so much in relation to vault design (although some are also covered with barrel vaults with lateral penetrations, like the one at Neuburg-an-der-Donau, for example), but because of the spectacular white stucco work that decorates their vaults: the motives are not the same as in Goa but the overall impression one has when observing the vaults is similar. Of course, vaults ornamented with stucco motives also appear in Belgian Jesuit churches, namely at the one in Namur.

The New Sacristy of Bom Jesus

The new sacristy of the Jesuit *Casa Professa* of the Bom Jesus is a stupendous piece of architecture, one of the finest sacristies I have ever seen anywhere in the world and certainly the best in Asia. Its plan consists of a double square 20m long by 10m wide, in modern linear measures. In volume up to the cornice it consists of a double cube. This rectangular based space is articulated length-wise into three bays by pilasters dividing the arches and windows into niches. The central bay is slightly wider than the other thus giving a centre to the

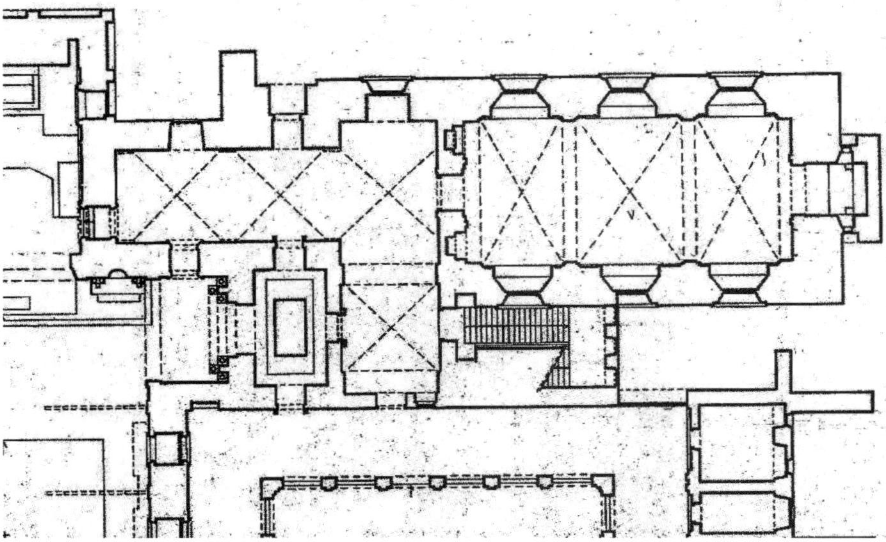

Bom Jesus, Old Goa, plan, detail of the sacristy, ante-sacristy and chapel of S.F.X.

Bom Jesus, Old Goa, sacristy, beg. 1652, vault

Bom Jesus, Old Goa, sacristy, lateral arch

longitudinal plan. The space is covered by a groin vault with lateral penetrations divided into three sections separated by arches, corresponding to the three bays. The windows under the penetrations are octagonal while the arches and niches are pentagonal. At the end opposite the entrance there is a chancel that constitutes one of the surprises of this surprising building: it is square in plan, very small, and it is covered by a semi-hemispherical dome supported by four shell-shaped triangular pendentifs in the corners. The dome itself is divided into four corresponding sections decorated as shells.

The white stucco decoration on the vaults, the wall order, the niches and the arches is quite spectacular: its motives are Flemish-type cartouches decorated with *rollwerk* and flowery forms, penetrations designed as fans, rope mouldings. This covers the arches, the coffers of the half-domes of the lateral niches and the dome of the chancel. It all looks like some architectural decoration used in Portugal precisely in the 1650s: the doors of the Loreto church in Lisbon, for instance or, more to the point, in the façade of the Jesuit church at Santarém, which was under construction at exactly that time.

The liturgical furniture and the painted decoration of the triumphal arch and of some cartouches are all well-preserved and give us a feeling of what the new sacristy must have

Bom Jesus, Old Goa, sacristy, chancel's dome

Bom Jesus, Old Goa, sacristy, detail of ornament

Bom Jesus, Old Goa, sacristy, view towards the chancel

felt like to its first visitors (only the blue and white *azulejos* at the chancel's main altar do not belong here, having been brought from the N.S. da Graça).

The new sacristy at Bom Jesus was begun in 1652 and was completed within a year, in 1653, although the overall campaign of works lasted until 1659 (Pissurlencar 1935). It was paid for by a Portuguese tradesman or nobleman residing in Goa, named Baltazar da Veiga, who was given a prominent burial site at the feet of the sacristy's altar: his tombstone, displaying the coat of arms of a *fidalgo*, informs us that he died in 1659.

The sacristy appears like a flash of lightning in a clear sky. No precedents in the architecture of Goa announce it. Unless I am completely deceived by the destruction of so many Goan churches in the 19th century, no vault like it had ever been built. No polygonal arches of this type, half-domes, windows. No decoration with ropes or fan-like motives (actually, the decoration and the use of polygonal forms were a one-off occasion and we never saw anything quite like that after the sacristy).

Who could have devised (and designed) such a building? It obviously did not come within the continuity of Jesuit architectural and artistic practice in Goa. I will come back to this authorship question in a while but it is my view that the unexpected nature of the sacristy can only be explained by the fact that it was part of what seems to have been a complete remodelling of the south wing of the *Casa Professa*.

The precise contours of this campaign of works that led to a profound change in the appearance and functions of the Bom Jesus are unknown to me, but I suspect that the Jesuits were gearing up the Professed House for what would become its then still-distant future: the shrine of St. Francis Xavier and the locus of his worship.

St. Francis Xavier was canonized in 1622 and a cenotaph was created in the Bom Jesus immediately after, between 1624 and 1637. The significant date of St. Francis worship, however, has always been considered to be the year 1683 when Viceroy Alvor dedicated to him the government of Portuguese India at the time when Goa was very seriously threatened by the Maratha (Francisco de Sousa IV, I, 107). It was after this, in 1697–98, that the Grand-Duke of Tuscany offered to the Bom Jesus the world famous Florentine funereal monument that constitutes the Basilica's artistic centrepiece.

However, this monument was installed in a chapel that was already in existence for four decades because it had been completed in 1659. The creation of that chapel, that is, the preparation of the Professed House for the worship of St. Francis was, I argue, the underlying motif behind the 1650s architectural reform, which seems to have literally rotated around that architectural space. The Jesuit 17th century document that describes the beginning and the programme of the work leaves no doubt that the sacristy with all its furnishings, the ante-sacristy (described as the *Via Sacra* 'that goes to the cloister and the church'), the staircase, the St. Francis chapel, were all planned and executed at the same time (Pissurlencar 1935).

The chapel was conceived not only to house but also to display the relics of the Saint: it is located at the extremity of the south arm of the transept and it is accessible through four open arches devised for the contemplation of people walking around it—similar in layout to a medieval tomb at the centre of a deambulatory. The chapel's main arch opens to the church via the extremity of the transept. The other arches open to new sections of the Professed House built at the same time as the chapel: one to the ante-sacristy, which is a wide corridor-like space covered by a barrel vault with lateral penetrations. A third opens to the passage to the cloister where the staircase is located and the fourth opens to the eastern arm of the cloister. To balance the new chapel, a Holy Sacrament chapel of the exact same dimensions was built against the northern arm of the transept (Nunes Pereira 2002: 223).

I am convinced that the existing *Portaria* of the Professed House was built in this same campaign over existing walls, as one can deduce by comparing the famous Valignano's drawings of the late 16th century and what exists now. It is a palazzo-like structure, which includes two reception rooms (the foundations of which existed already) as well as a

Bom Jesus Professed House ante-sacristy, view of the vault

new staircase behind a three-storey high, four-bay wide façade. It stands there in startling contrast to the older original late 16th-century building, which is so much simpler in appearance.

The Theatine Intervention

As the *Casa Professa* was thus being profoundly remodelled, an entirely new church building by a new religious order contributed to the increasing surprise of Goan society in the 1650s with things architectural. The church of Nossa Senhora da Divina Providência (Our Lady of Divine Providence or St. Cajetan) in Old Goa is an Italian building designed by Italian priests of an Italian congregation (the Theatines) after the central Italian architectural tradition and with the political and religious purpose of looking Italian. The dates and names of this church's design and construction have been established by Rafael Moreira in 1997. Construction began in 1656 and, with the exception of the western façade, was finished six years later, in 1661.

N.S. da Divina Providência (1656-1661), Old Goa, seen from the Mandovi river

The Theatines, or *Clerici Regolari della Divina Providenza*, were a religious congregation founded by Caetano de Thiene at the beginning of the 16th century for the preaching among the urban elite in Catholic Reformation Italy. They arrived in Goa in 1639 on their way to the kingdoms of the Deccan, in the interior of India, where they desired to play a role in the context of the *Propaganda Fide*'s evangelization drive in Asian territories outside the reach of the Portuguese *Padroado*.

While some of them went as far as Golconda and Bijapur in present-day Karnataka, others remained in Goa and asked for the Portuguese crown's permission to have a *Casa* (a conventual house) and church here. It took 15 years to obtain that authorization because of suspicions aroused by their allegiance to the *Propaganda* and to the fact that the Portuguese crown was at war with the Spanish and had its religious and political links with Rome severely threatened by the inclination of the Papacy in favour of Spain. The Theatines were thus suspected of being doubly hostile to the Portuguese crown: they were supported both by the *Propaganda* and by the Pope.

The Theatine's Italian chronicle reveals that the first and foremost sponsor of the Theatine church in Goa was the same Baltazar da Veiga (Moreira 1997) who had just paid for the new Sacristy at the Bom Jesus completed three years before. The biography of Baltazar da Veiga is not established. But this Goan Mecaenas deserves to be rescued from the relative oblivion of his secluded resting place at the Bom Jesus: he had both the means and the taste to sponsor the two more important architectural enterprises of Goa in the 17th century, those that would shape the destiny of Goan architecture.

I can now return to the issue of the identity of the Bom Jesus sacristy's architect that I left unresolved earlier: I think he was the same man who designed the Theatine church. The pivotal role played by Baltazar da Veiga in both buildings and the fact that these are totally new and unexpected in Goan architecture, leads me to that conviction. Rafael Moreira has established that the Theatine's designer was D. Carlo Ferrarini, the head of the Theatine mission in Goa, a priest born in Reggio Emilia in central Italy. The master mason who supervised the building process of the church was the lay brother Francesco (Francisco in Portuguese) Maria Milazzo. These two men had probably arrived in Goa not with the first Theatines in 1639 but rather a decade later in 1650 (Caetano do Bem: I, 150–153). Baltazar da Veiga and the Jesuits probably met Ferrarini, the designer, and Milazzo, the mason, when they were contemplating a sumptuous and innovative new project for the Professed House in 1650–51.

That a new way of thinking about architecture was spreading through Goan society is also indicated by the fact that the first thing that Veiga sponsored in the building process of the Theatine church was a painting showing the design of the façade of the future building as well as a wooden model of 'half the church', i.e., a section of the church, probably a longitudinal one (Moreira 1997). The painting and model represented a *mostra* of the building. It seems obvious that this *mostra* was made to raise awareness among the cognoscenti in Goa of the importance of what was going to be built and also to guide inexperienced workers in the erection of the new system of vaults and dome, which Goa had never seen. Façade and architectural *parti* for vaults and dome, after all the true innovations of the Theatine design, were thus clearly presented in Goa from 1656 onwards.

Divina Providência is a centralized plan church of the Theatine type. However, primarily at the beginning of the order's history, the model chosen for their churches by the Theatines was that of the Roman Jesuits. An example would be the Theatine's mother church, Sant'Andrea della Valle in Rome, begun by Giacomo Della Porta in 1591 and continued by Carlo Maderno after 1608, because it is a longitudinal church very much like the Jesuit's *Gesú* near which it is located. But the first design for that church foresaw a quincunx church, i.e., a square plan with an inscribed Greek cross covered with six domes (Hibbard 1961). In northern and central Italy the Theatine churches are of this type, also chosen for Goa: the model for Divina Providência was the church of Madonna della Ghiara at Reggio, the hometown of father Ferrarini, a quincunx type of

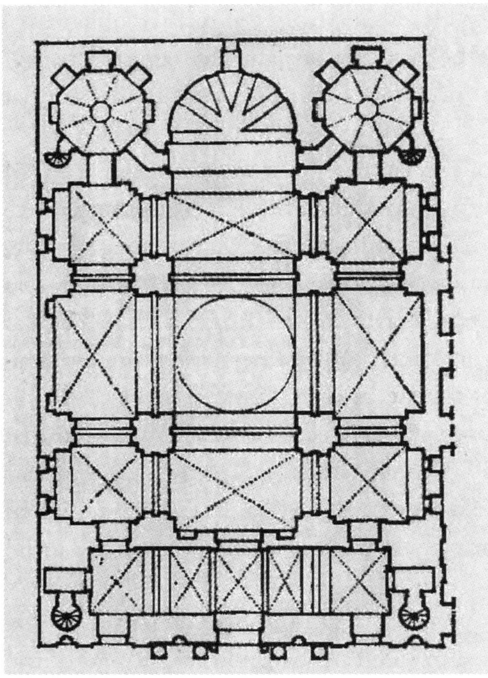

N.S. da Divina Providência, Old Goa, plan (DGEMN, Lisbon)

church. St. Peter's in Rome is often mentioned in connection with Divina Providência, but its plan and volume originate in the central and northern Italian tradition (a tradition which, incidentally, also stands at the roots of St. Peter's itself, design by Bramante and Michelangelo).

The Goan Theatine church is the only large centrally planned church covered by a complete dome with drum and lantern to have been built in Portuguese Asia. Its plan is square. By bringing down the square's diagonal one creates the space for the chancel and the two octagonal divisions at its sides. These divisions also have domes with drums and lanterns, thus joining two minor domes to the central one, in a clear evocation of the quincunx principle. The narthex with the façade, built later in 1673 (Moreira 1997), increases the overall plan to a double square.

The church's central dome rests upon four big arches that, in their turn, are supported by massive square pillars faced by four Composite order pilasters by pillar. The corner spaces, which are lower than the central Greek cross, are articulated by an attic order.

The four arms of the central Greek cross are covered with rectangular groin vaults between arches, one per arm, decorated with stuccoed lozenge coffers. The four corner spaces also display groin vaults, square in plan, with stuccoed octagonal coffers. The chancel is covered by

N.S. da Divina Providência, Old Goa, interior with dome

an extraordinary semi-hemispherical vault, torn by penetrations, much like a gothic ribbed vault. The rich carving of the pilaster's fluting and of its frankly exaggerated capitals, of the friezes, coffers and arches, and the fact that all of this is uniformly whitewashed, enhances the variations in luminosity of the interior.

Entering the church of Divina Providência for the first time must have been a truly dramatic revelation for the clergy, the *fidalgos* and the people of Goa: here was something the like of which they had never experienced, something truly extraordinary, something for which not even the sacristy of the Bom Jesus could have prepared them.

However this aesthetic revolution was only a part of a deeper and more complex change of the perception of things, architectural and otherwise, induced by the action of the Theatines in Goa. In fact, the Italian Theatine priests' architectural enterprise in Goa is inseparable from their evangelical intervention, which had a significant impact upon Goan society—an impact undoubtedly reinforcing and in turn being reinforced by their novel architecture. Seven years after their arrival in Goa, in January 1646, the Theatines presented a series of public conferences in the Sé Cathedral about the possibility of the Holy Communion being administered to the Indian Christians at least in Easter and for the Last Rites (Nazaré 149 ff). The preacher was the first Theatine leader and spokesman in Goa, the Neapolitan

N.S. da Divina Providência, Old Goa, chancel

Antonio Ardizone Spinola (1609–97) who was later to become the *Preposito* of the Theatines in Lisbon and play a key role in important episodes of the history of European architecture (Klaiber 1993; P.V. Gomes 2003; 2006).

This is not the occasion to elaborate upon matters of Christian liturgy and ritual but in the 17th century, the Holy Communion was not as commonly-administered a Sacrament as it is today. However, the fact that it was not made available to non-Europeans in Portuguese India was considered unacceptable by the Theatines and by many other people within the Catholic Church, including some among the Portuguese themselves. The reform suggested by the Theatine preacher was in fact approved for all of India although its implementation did face a lot of resistance.

This story has never been investigated as it deserves to be. But it seems to me that Ardizone Spinola chose this particular issue in order to confront the Goan ecclesiastical status quo because he was pursuing the mixed agenda of the *Propaganda Fide* and the native clergy in Portuguese-influenced India, especially the clergy of Brahmin origin, to which I referred in the Introduction. The title of Spinola's famous Sermon in Goa's *Sé* gives the Brahmins due prominence: *Gemido dos Christãos bremanes e canarins e de muitas outras castas e nações do estado da India por não comungarem em nenhum tempo de vida* (Lamentation of the Christian

N.S. da Divina Providência, Old Goa, view from the Monte

brahmin and cannari and of many other castes and nations of the state of India for not being administered communion in any time of their lives, Lisbon, 1656).

The blatant, even aggressive, Italianism in the architecture of the church of Divina Providência is an obvious declaration of difference. The Theatine chronicle states that their order wanted to have a building "all'italiana" and with "insolita architettura". The main objective was to raise a "superbissima Cupola (cosa insolita nelle Indie)", a superb dome, a thing unheard of in India. The dome of Divina Providência, the architectural crowning of Old Goa's now impoverished skyline, was conceived and built as a statement—and as such, the Theatines desired that it should be clearly understood. Only then did Goa truly earn the title of Rome of the East that was later attributed to the city.

And then, at last, came the façade. It was built between 1673 and 1675, also very quickly. The chronicle describes it as a 'brief but well executed' compêndio 'of everything one can see in the façade of the church of St. Peter in Rome', a remark ceaselessly repeated ever since in all tones and by everybody, the word *compêndio* being translated as copy. It is however not exactly a copy of St. Peter: *compêndio* actually means something like a summary, an abstract. St. Peter's façade is much, much wider (and higher, that goes without saying). Divina Providência's façade is articulated by a pilastered giant order, it has a columnar portico at

N.S. da Divina Providência, Old Goa, view from the west

the centre crowned by a triangular pediment and a pilastered attic running above the whole length, all similar to St. Peter's. But differently from St. Peter's it has two towers springing from the attic.

It is generally known how Bernini tried to solve the complex problem of the articulation of Maderno's attic with his own towers at St. Peter's. In Goa, the solution escaped the designer. His towers look like an option out of a catalogue of available Italian examples: in this instance those of the church of Trinitá dei Monti, in Rome, with one floor, pediment, attic and lantern. But unlike the Roman examples, the Goan towers have no continuity whatsoever with the rest of the façade.

Built more than ten years after the church was completed, the façade of Divina Providência is definitely awkward. The designer's intention—probably Milazzo—was to create a replica of St. Peter's in the centre of Goa, practically adjacent to the Viceroy's palace. It was no longer enough for the Theatines to have an Italian church; they needed St. Peter's itself.

Furthermore they needed a monumental façade for their church, which would simultaneously respond to the architectural skyline of Goa: they had introduced the dome to the *Velha Cidade* but they also wanted towers like those of the cathedral and the Augustinians on the hill. Unfortunately the façade and the towers hide the view of the dome for any

Trinitá dei Monti, Rome (concl. 1585), view of towers

observer stationed in front of the church, a classical problem of domed churches and their façades that no Goan Bernini was able to solve (at the time).

The Holy Sacrament Chapel at the Sé

The Theatines' insistence on the cult of the Eucharist probably influenced the creation of the Holy Sacrament confraternity at the Cathedral in 1647, the first of this invocation in Goa (Rocha 1973: 26). This confraternity must have triggered the construction of the chapel dedicated to the Eucharist, which was added to the south flank of the Sé. João Pereira Mourato, a priest from Santarém, Portugal, patronized the chapel (*Memória* 1933: 196–97), but this does not necessarily mean that he paid for its construction. Fr. Pereira Mourato died in 1652 and is buried at the entrance of the chapel. Prior to this time, the Holy Sacrament was likely kept in a tabernacle in the main altar because, unlike other 16th-century Portuguese Cathedrals, Goa's Cathedral does not have lateral transept chapels one of which customarily housed the Holy Sacrament. It is also possible that the new Communion habits induced by the Theatine's preaching raised the need for a place for the worship and administration of the Eucharist away from the main altar and the Cathedral canons choir placed there.

Cathedral, Old Goa, Holy Sacrament chapel, mid 17th century

The new construction resembles a little church attached to the Cathedral's body: the openings connecting the lateral chapels along the southern aisle were closed so that one of the chapels, the third counting from the western façade could function as the nave of the Holy Sacrament chapel. Emerging from the flank of the Cathedral, a rectangular transept, brightly illuminated by two windows placed at ground level, leads to the chamber housing the tabernacle and the throne of the Eucharist. This chamber communicates with another one of the exact same plan and volume (respectively a square and a cube) placed perpendicular to it towards the west, which functions as a kind of sacristy. Its purpose is to house the Eucharist in between services. The two main chambers, and the Cathedral's lateral chapel that serves as the 'nave' of the Holy Sacrament chapel, are covered by square penetration barrel vaults and the 'transept' by a barrel vault. These vaults are lavishly articulated by stucco coffers and richly painted in golden tones.

The south-turned façades of the Holy Sacrament chambers display octagonal oculi at the upper level, the only case of polygonal openings in Old Goa apart from the sacristy at the Bom Jesus and another indicator, together with the type of the vaults and their stucco and painting decoration, that the chapel is one of the key buildings of the 1650s in Old Goa.

Cathedral, Old Goa, Holy Sacrament chapel and its vestry seen from the south

THE FRANCISCAN CHURCH IN VELHA GOA

So far, the new buildings were two structures added to older constructions - the sacristy at Bom Jesus, the Holy Sacrament chapel at the Sé, and a complete church, Divina Providência, of a type so new that it made it difficult to appropriate or imitate. But a 'normal' church soon appeared, which displayed all the possibilities of the new vaulting system: the renovation, begun in 1661, of the early 16th-century Holy Spirit church of the Franciscan's convent in Old Goa. Its main feature was the truly remarkable vault built over the nave and its false transept: five narrow rectangular groin vaults between planed arches, decorated with square stucco coffers. And over the deep chancel two rectangular groin vaults. This alone would have required an architect or a master builder with great skills, well acquainted with the complex vaulting system of Divina Providência, which was completed precisely in that very same year of 1661. The very plane groin vault under the entrance choir is particularly ambitious.

The church was located along a narrow street, replaced in modern times by the large empty terrain, and in the late 1950s by the absurd garden-like setting that we see today. Taking advantage of the new vaulting system, the architect placed all the windows at high levels along the nave leaving blank the lower part of the outside wall, which fell on the

Church of Espírito Santo, Franciscan convent, Old Goa, beg. 1661, view towards the entrance

street. The higher row of windows was opened between the buttresses corresponding to the arches of the vault. These windows are responsible for the clarity of the Espírito Santo's vaults and of its interior luminosity. Below these, other windows were opened above the arches corresponding to the lateral chapels and they were described as *janelas de sacada* (windows with balconies), a solution quite typical of several Goan churches. Those on the southern flank open to the convent cloister's upper gallery, while those on the northern flank are linked by a corridor-like gallery coming from the upper choir and running above the lateral chapels.

I believe, along with Rafael Moreira (1997), that the designer of the church's renovation was Francesco Maria Milazzo, the man who had conducted the building of the Theatine church begun six years before. In fact, the Theatine's chronicle states that Milazzo abandoned the Italian order and went over to the Franciscan convent where he was ordained a priest. This is unconfirmed information but the similarities between the two buildings appear to be undeniable.

An entirely new façade was built incorporating the Manueline door of the original church. The façade is as awkward as that of the Theatine's albeit for different reasons: here the architect was faced not with the need to imitate St. Peter's but rather with a type of narrow

Church of Espírito Santo, Old Goa, view from the south

Church of Espírito Santo, Old Goa, detail of frontal façade

and high late Medieval church for which the repertoire of the current mid 17th century façade forms offered no clear-cut solution. He resorted to a palatial composition in which the proportions of windows, the form of pediments and balusters, as well as the treatment of many pilasters all recall the façade of Divina Providência.

And then he crowned the whole thing with two small octagonal towers, the likes of which appear nowhere else in Goan or Portuguese architecture. As we shall see in the coming chapter, there were to be quite a few octagonal church towers or octagonal tower cupolas built in Goan churches in the first half of the 18th century (although the strange towers of Old Goa's Franciscans have remained unique in their specific form).

David Kowal offered the only interesting explanation I have read for this proliferation of the octagonal tower. Drawing our attention to the fact that the octagonal form was also profusely used in the 18th century by the builders of Hindu temples in territories under Maratha influence, which would later be incorporated into Portuguese Goa, David Kowal explained this as due to the influence of the architecture of the more important political and cultural centre of the Deccan in the second half of the 17th century: the sultanate of Bijapur. In fact, Bijapuri 17th-century mosques and tombs incorporate many octagonal towers and domes and the extraordinary quantity and quality of these prestigious buildings commissioned by the Adil Shahis of Bijapur must have had some impact in South India. It is

Gol Gumbaz, Bijapur, concl. 1656

very likely that they were well known in Goa. European ambassadors, merchants and artists travelled to Bijapur frequently. The Bijapuri court was highly cosmopolitan, cultivated and open to people of all creeds.

But, that having been said, is it really conceivable that the Franciscans chose to deliberately use forms that were related to Bijapur in the main façade of their renovated mother church in Goa? I think so. As we already know, and as strange as it may seem to our contemporary minds, trained in the ideologies of religious extremism and of clear-cut differences between 'civilizations', in the 1650s the kingdom of Bijapur played a key role in the complex situation of Catholicism in Goa.

An interesting aspect of the Franciscan's church, which is new compared to the original early 16th-century structure but which was probably added to the church later in that century and maintained in the 1661 renovation, and, furthermore, which has received very little attention despite its overwhelming visual impact in the interior of the church, is the *camarin* designed to provide rear lighting to the Holy Sacrament tabernacle in the main altar. I have already briefly referred to this type of chambers housing the tabernacle when speaking about the church of the Augustinians in Old Goa.

Church of Espírito Santo, Old Goa, main altar and camarin

Camarins

Triggered by the Catholic Reformation's emphasis on the worship of the Holy Sacrament, architectural ideas for prominently displaying the tabernacle of the Eucharist occurred to a number of European architects and patrons. The most elegant, albeit not the more commonly used, was of an altar accessible from both sides, choir and nave, with a large tabernacle designed as a centrally planned small church under an open arch at its centre. This was tried out with great artistic success by many architects. The name of Andrea Palladio obviously comes to mind with his two famous monastic Venetian churches of San Giorgio Maggiore (1561) and Il Redentore (1571) where the friars' choir is placed behind the altar, the latter having two faces, one to the congregation, another to the choir.

In the nations of the Iberian Peninsula the choir behind the altar was never a popular idea, although three were installed in Portugal: very high and wide altars with polygonal tabernacles placed in an open arch occupy the eastern extremity of the naves separating the laity from the choir at the monastic churches of N.S. da Luz at Carnide (begun in 1574), S. Vicente de Fora (1583) and S. Domingos de Benfica (1624), all in or near Lisbon. The fact that the choir behind the altar arrangement of the Augustinian mother church of S. Vicente de Fora was not adopted in the order's church in Goa, N.S. da Graça, clearly demonstrates the reluctance of the Iberian clergy in adopting a retro-choir solution.

The need for a 'transparent' altar, visible to both the congregation placed in front of the altar as well as from other parts of the church reserved for the clergy, was addressed in several other architectural solutions, one of which is the *camarin* (the word is Castilian, there is no translation to Portuguese), a chamber, often very small, placed behind the altar and opened to the exterior of the church by a window or windows, the main purpose of which is to retro-illuminate the tabernacle, in a disposition that could have been inspired by theatre settings.

Sometimes a chapel specially dedicated to the Holy Sacrament was built right behind the chancel and open to it from behind. These chapels, however, known as *Sagrarios* or *Capillas Sacramentales,* did not function as *camarins* because the tabernacle was not visible from the nave. The chapels' only purpose was to keep the Holy Host between services. This was the case in the spectacular and world-famous *Sagrarios* at the Cartouchian Spanish monasteries of Granada and El Paular (Segovia), but also many others, more frequent than one might think, in both Spanish and French large churches.

Camarins have been surveyed, described and documented in the case of the architecture of the several regions of Spain. But to my knowledge there is not a single study dedicated to their use in Portugal itself. And yet *camarins* exist everywhere from north to south Portugal, built in new churches or added to old churches from the second half of the 16th century onwards.

Church of Espírito Santo, Old Goa, view from the east

And, not surprisingly, they exist in Portuguese India too. The *camarin* and transparent altar of the Franciscan's Espírito Santo achieves its impact because of its extraordinary architectural refinement. The altar is in fact the wood-facing of the ending wall of the church's chancel. Behind it, the architect placed a rectangular, narrow and high building divided into a basement and two floors and into three compartments length-wise. The central chamber is the *camarin* behind the altar, in the middle of which the tabernacle is placed. It offers a large round arched window to the eastern morning light. The staircase giving access to the *camarin* is placed in the compartment to the north of it.

In Bassein, the northern Portuguese capital, at the church of the Franciscan convent of Santo António, one of the better preserved ruins of the ruined city, one can still see the *camarin* open towards the chancel by an arch placed high on the back wall, a solution exactly like the one at Goa. The convent was founded in 1547 but the church was remodelled in the transition between the 16th and the 17th centuries and it was probably then that the *camarin* was built. The Jesuit church in Bassein also had a *camarin* and so did the Dominican church in Daman. The idea was quite popular in the former *Província do Norte*, it seems.

The Augustinian church of Nossa Senhora da Graça in Old Goa, built between 1602 and 1620 also had a *camarin*. Its archaeological remains can still be found in the site, a

Church of Santo António, Franciscan convent, Bassein, view of the chancel

reconstitution of its form was attempted (Mendiratta 2004), and early descriptions leave no doubt about it being a barrel vault-covered small chamber placed behind the altar.

An altar and *camarin,* which imitated the Franciscan church at Old Goa was built after 1681 in the church of Santana de Talaulim, and a little later in the church of Piedade at Divar, to which I will return later in this chapter. The Franciscan's church in Bardez, Reis Magos (The Magi Kings), also has a *camarin.* The existing building is 18th-century, the product of an extensive architectural transformation of an older structure. The *camarin* is a replica of the one in Old Goa adapted to a different topography: the church is built on an ascending slope and the tabernacle and *camarin* could therefore be placed level with the altar. The *camarin* is a deep corridor-like room illuminated sideways from the south. It is likely that the original 16th-century church also had a *camarin.* The Reis Magos convent had the first 17th-century *Confraria* (Confraternity) of the Holy Sacrament to have been created in Bardez (Rocha 1973), and the *camarin* almost certainly existed then.

The more conspicuous Franciscan *camarin* in Goa is located at the church of S. Jerónimo in Mapuça. It has a tower raised over it, the only tower of the church, and it makes Mapuça the earliest church in Goa with a tower placed on the axis of the chancel thus causing the puzzlement of many observers who are not used to this type of church in Catholic India. It

Reis Magos, Bardez, interior: 18th century, view of the chancel and the camarin

is popularly suggested that the tower would have been the result of the influence of Hindu temples with their towers over the shrine but the prosaic truth is that the tower-behind-the-chancel solution was fairly common in Northern Portugal in the 18th century; one need only recall the famous tower behind the chancel in the church of Clérigos in Porto.

S. Jerónimo de Mapuça's chancel was built anew by Archbishop D. frei Francisco de Assunção e Brito between 1775 and 1778 with these Portuguese precedents in mind. But, of course, there probably was a Franciscan *camarin* in the existing church and the Archbishop chose to reinforce its meaning by having the tower placed on it. The present-day existing altar, brought from the convent of Madre de Deus in Daugim in the 19th century, prevents the reading of the chancel's original appearance and the image of Our Lady of Miracles is now placed in the arch that opened to the *camarin*.

The tower-behind-the-chancel solution was copied in 1836 at the church of Moirá, also in Bardez (*Memória* 1933: 253), for purely formal reasons having nothing to do with the existence of a *camarin*. The Moirá church had been going through extensive remodelling since the early years of the century. The new tower's purpose was to serve a massive bell brought from the Jesuit's church of S. Roque in Old Goa and there is no *camarin* below it.

S. Jerónimo, Mapuça, 1775–1778, view from the west

The number and importance of Franciscan *camarins* in India shows that Indian Franciscans favoured a Spanish type of cult of the Holy Sacrament. The reasons for this are unknown to me although I do know that the same thing does not happen in Franciscan architecture in Portugal. I hope that future historians of religion will be able to explain this anomaly to us.

The Jesuit Church at Margão

The Jesuit church of the Espírito Santo (Holy Spirit) in Margão presents a complex problem for architectural historians, the solving of which could be of great importance for the understanding of what happened in Goan architecture in the 17th century: the Jesuit chronicles speak of a process of destruction and reconstruction of this church, the Jesuits' more important house in south Goa (besides their fortified settlement of Rachol). Apparently the church was first built in 1564–65, a date in accordance with the Jesuit arrival in Salcete. In 1571 the church seems to have been at least partially destroyed by fire as a consequence of the raid by Bijapur and its allies, and the same happened again in 1579. A reconstruction then took place between 1585 (or 1589) and 1595, in a slightly different location. This building would have been 'augmented', whatever this means, in 1604 (these data are from the Jesuit chronicle by Francisco de Sousa written in Goa in 1698). Half a century later in

Espírito Santo, Margão, uncertain dates (1585? 1645?)

1645, says the same chronicle, *se derrubou toda a fabrica velha e se fez no mesmo lugar a igreja de que hoje usamos, toda de abobada, muito clara e aprazivel* (I, I, 7): 'the old church was completely pulled down and the church we now use was built in the same site, all vaulted, very well illuminated and pleasant.' This would have taken 30 years to complete because the church was consecrated only in 1675.

In the late 1580s, as we have seen in Chapter 2, Catholic architecture was going through a true revolution in Goa under the influence of Júlio Simão and Jesuit architecture was part of this profound change. In this context, it is necessary to ask what the church of Espírito Santo concluded in 1595 would have looked like. Would it have been of the type of the Bom Jesus and of the church of the Seminary of Rachol, for instance, its exact Jesuit contemporaries, very large and very high single nave churches covered by wooden roofs?

This would be a safe assumption if it weren't for a a problem: the church existing in Margão displays one unexpected and important typological aspect, so important that it would later become one of the more conspicuous, albeit less noticed, signs of the 'Goaness' of Goan Catholic architecture: the semi-circular lateral niches sheltering door or windows and covered with shell-shaped semi-domes that we see articulating the lower lateral order. We know of no earlier church in Goa with this type of plan.

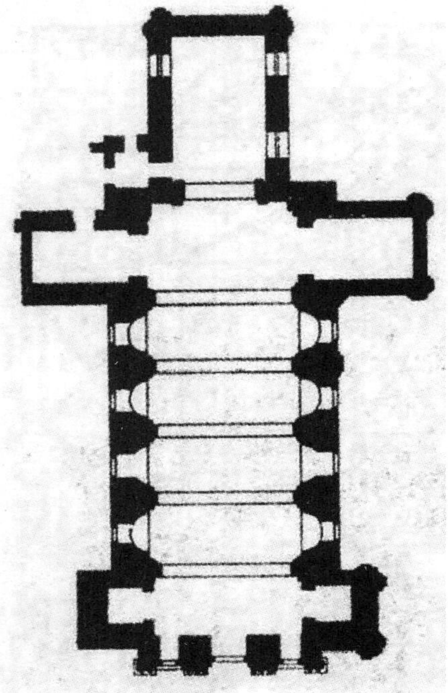

Espírito Santo, Margão, plan (drawing by M.T. Chicó)

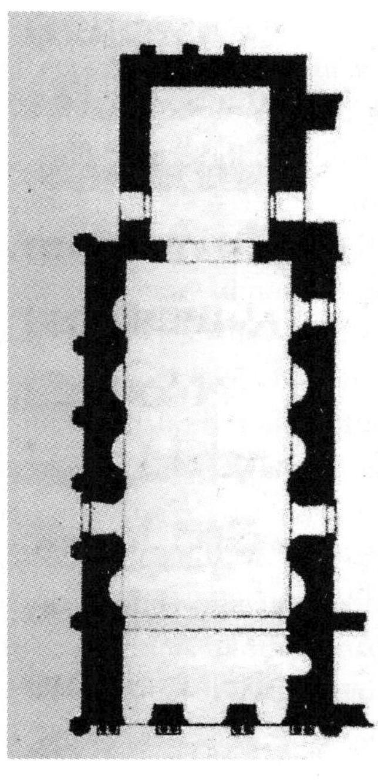

N.S. da Conceição or S. Paulo, Diu, beg. 1601, plan (drawing by M.T. Chicó)

Semi-circular side niches can however be seen somewhere else: at the church of Nossa Senhora da Conceição (Our Lady of Conception), also known as S. Paulo (St. Paul), in Diu. They articulate a nave covered with a barrel vault. The first stone of S. Paulo was laid on 7 April 1601. The design was by the Jesuit priest Gaspar Soares (Rivara 1865: 41), who later founded the Seminary of Rachol in 1605.

The articulation of church naves by niche-shaped spaces is a theme that appears to have been created by the Florentine architect Filippo Bruneleschi in his project for the basilica of Santo Spirito in Florence at the beginning of the 15th century. The theme had very little success in Italian and generally in European architectural culture: semi-circular chapels (not niches) appeared in some buildings and drawings by the architect Francesco di Giorgio Martini, and also at some Roman churches like Santo Agostino, Holy Spirit in Sassia, and S. Pietro in Montorio among others, the latter famous for its Bramante's little temple (*tempietto*) in the middle of the cloister rather than for its nave. Subsequently the theme was picked up by the Italian Sebastiano Serlio for a plan for a three nave church printed in his architectural treatise (Book V, published 1547 in Paris).

Lateral semi-circular niches or chapels do not exist in Portuguese architecture in either Portugal or Brazil. To my knowledge, there is not a single case. There are isolated niched

N.S. da Conceição or S. Paulo, Diu, interior

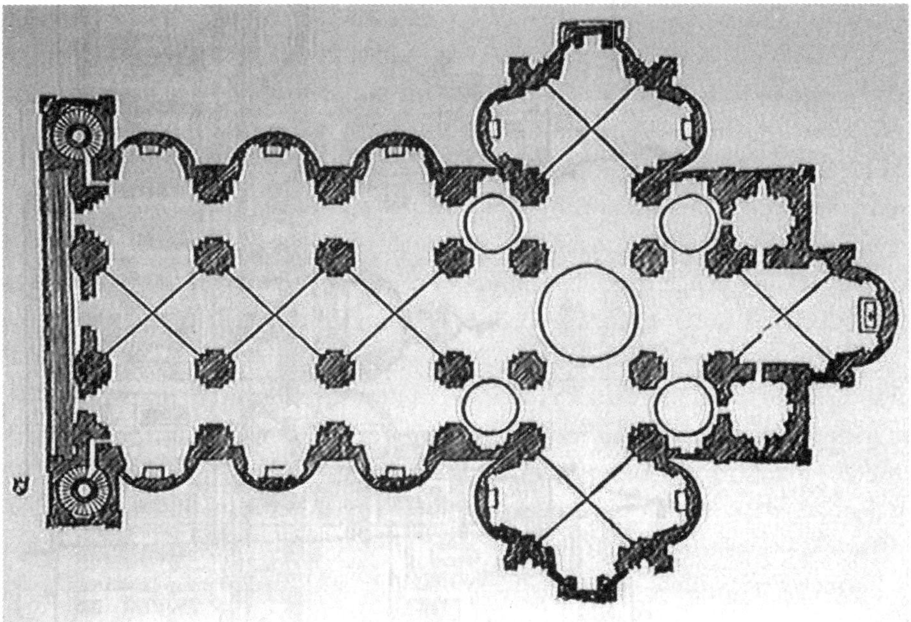

Plan for a three nave church, Sebastiano Serlio, Book V, 1547 Paris

chapels: one hard-to-interpret chapel in the main parish church, later Cathedral, in Viana do Castelo, a lone cloister chapel at the convent of Lóios in Arraiolos, both 16th-century cases, but that's about it.

I don't know that the theme appeared in Spanish or Flemish architectures either. It is consequently a very rare theme. However, it was not wholly strange to Jesuit culture. The Society's church in Munich, South Germany, dedicated to Saint Michael and built between 1583 and 1597, has semi-circular topped lateral chapels that, although not exactly following the Bruneleschi and Serlio prototype because only the end-wall is curved and not the whole perimeter of the chapel, show that Munich Jesuits knew Serlio's treaty, and possibly drawings representing Bruneleschi's never realised intentions for an undulating exterior for his basilica in correspondence with the round chapels. This is less of a far-fetched hypothesis as it might seem at first sight, if one bears in mind that the east side elevation of Saint Michael giving onto the street (the opposite side is taken by the college) does indeed reveal the curved walls of the chapels.

Semi-circular niches were frequently used in the micro-architecture of wooden altars where we can see many with their shell-shaped half-domes. A case in point is the series of altars of the Santa Mónica church in Old Goa, dating from the early years of the 17th century; or in the lateral altars in the chapel of Nossa Senhora do Monte, also of the same period. It is very likely that the beauty of the shell-shaped domes over tabernacle niches in altars, with all their Marian overtones (the shell is a well-known symbol of Our Lady), would have impressed Jesuit Goan architects.

Therefore I suggest that the theme of a nave articulated by semi-circular niches was invented by the Jesuits in India and for India although it is very hard to believe that it appeared isolated in a far away place like Diu in 1601. Must it not have been tried out at the same time in other Jesuit churches in Goa?

A likely solution to this riddle would be that the church of S. Paulo in Goa, the Jesuit's first in India (which was a three-nave church) had one semi-circular chapel at each side of the main chapel (Jesuit documents inform that the church had a three-chapel chancel). In the S. Paulo façade's remains, there are two semi-circular niches with shell-shaped vaults on both sides of the window above the main door (where in the past the statues of St. Peter and St. Paul probably stood). But there is another possibility: perhaps the semi-circular niches were introduced to the church of Margão itself when it was rebuilt between 1585 and 1595.

At the end of the 19th century one could still see in the church three tombstones of gaunkars from Margão dated 1618, 1620 and 1648 and located directly under the windows,

Altar, N.S. do Monte, early 17th century

in the semi-circular recesses of the nave. Recent wooden flooring now hides the tombstones. Two other tombstones exist, of the same epoch but without inscription, totalling five, all in the window recesses. When these tombs were described at the end of the 19th century (Gracias 1893) all other tombs in the church were modern and they were located in the middle of the nave or in the crossing (these modern tombs corresponded to a new paving of the church).

It seems highly unlikely that tombs prior to 1645—the date at which the church would have been 'completely pulled down' as father Francisco de Sousa put it—were reinstalled in a new church, especially in places so particularly located as the recesses of the lateral niches.

Tentatively I would submit that the basic form of Margão's church is the one laid in the 1580s. In favour of this hypothesis I would add that the vaults and mouldings of the arches of the two chapels corresponding to the towers, as well as the pediments and pilasters of these towers, appear to resemble late 16th- or early 17th-century works.

I understand that my suggestion is contrary to father Francisco de Sousa's claim that the church built in the 1580s was *toda derrubada*, completely pulled down, but I note that this phrase was a *topos* of renovating patrons everywhere in the pre-modern and early modern worlds who naturally liked preferred new to old buildings. My reading is that the

Espírito Santo, Margão,
detail of arch and vault of the chapel under the north tower

Espírito Santo, Margão, interior, vaulting after 1645

church was profoundly repaired, with the vault of the chancel being replaced, the nave and transept vaulted for the first time, the façades, internal and, partly, external, being redone, the decoration being upgraded.

The chancel's covering is a barrel vault with no arches and only lateral penetrations. Over the nave a spectacular barrel vault with lateral penetrations was built: five narrow rectangular vaults between arches with very ornamented rectangular coffers cover it corresponding to the five bays of the nave (one of which is under the upper choir). The church has a real transept, an uncommon typological trait in Goan architecture. A groin vault covers the crossing. The transept has no spatial expression in the nave because its arches are low and of approximately the same width as the nave's niches.

As far as the vaults are concerned we are far from the almost gothic elegance and daring of the Franciscans in Old Goa but the sought after novelty celebrated by padre Francisco de Sousa was achieved: the architect has indeed designed a church 'all vaulted, very well illuminated and pleasant', in fact one of the more luminous and pleasant interiors of Goan Catholic architecture.

The building's nave is articulated by a giant order of fluted pilasters with a Doric frieze under an Ionic architrave supported by curved mensole similar to the ones seen at the

Espírito Santo, Margão, transept arch

Espírito Santo, Margão, detail of the order

Cathedral in Old Goa. Separated by the pilasters, the niches display this same system. A sculpted shell-like vault crowns each niche and we can see here the same brilliant naturalism of the vault of the *Casa Professa*'s sacristy. Metopae, coffers and several types of frames display delicate flowery decoration. This is the best ornamental sculpture to be found in any church in Goa, even surpassing the Theatine interior. The lesson of the sacristy at the *Casa Professa* and of the Theatines was well learned: subtle sculpture bathed in white and in light has produced incredibly beautiful space with an apparent simplicity of means.

The western façade is of the Augustinian N.S. da Graça type: a central part divided into three orders sided by two slightly withdrawn four-order towers capped by small domes with lanterns. The columns are all of the Composite order although the entablature is Ionic like the order inside the nave. The façade's central decoration is later in character and looks to be the work of someone trained in the fabrication of wooden altars: the columns and their capitals are just like pieces of *talha*: the pilasters are too wide and short, the ornamental sculpture is coarser. We are far from the delicacy of the interior. The façade's top pediment is obviously a later addition.

The central part of the façade represents a departure from the architecturally controlled design of mouldings that prevailed in Goa until then and we see a more sculptural and

Espírito Santo, Margão, detail of the façade

decorative conception of the use of architectural orders and of ornaments. Filled up areas dominate and there is a clear preference for the concentration of sculptural motives. Proportions of architectural members derived from architectural treatises are lost: pilasters and columns get short and fat.

This evolution in style is sometimes interpreted as having been caused by the influence of Indian workmanship and Indian taste but the evidence available both in Europe and in India leads me to disagree because an identical evolution took place in Portugal and Spain in the same epoch. I believe the real reason for the change, besides a shift in sensibility usually described as the evolution toward Baroque, is the fact that sculptors of altars increasingly became designers of buildings in the transition between the 17th and the 18th centuries. Of course, in Goa these sculptors were, in fact, Goan and consequently their training and tastes can well account for the type of ornamentation, for the motives and for the choice of proportions that dominated the articulation of elevations in Goa.

Santo António and the Sacristy of Nossa Senhora do Carmo at Old Goa

A vault with penetrations was built circa 1680 in the chancel of the old chapel of Santo António at the *Monte Santo* in Old Goa which had been under Augustinian care since

Santo António, Old Goa, chancel's vault, ca. 1680

Ruins of the convent of the Carmelites, Old Goa (photo Sousa & Paul)

the early 17th century: a barrel vault with lateral penetrations, decorated with magnificent stucco motives, integrating all the vocabulary that had been used in Old Goa and Margão over the previous 30 years and probably many that existed next door at Nossa Senhora da Graça and have subsequently disappeared with the monumental church's collapse: shells, flowers, stripes.

The church of the Carmelites built in the first half of the 17th century is another possible interesting case of the application of the new types of vaulting as we have already noted in the previous chapter. One of the Sousa & Paul photographs of the ruins shows the remains of another very interesting vault in the Carmelite convent which, judging by the more accurate of the *Velha Cidade* plans traced in 1777, was located above a room to the north of the chancel and was as high as the nave of the church itself. It probably was a sacristy, rectangular in plan, very high and, as shown by the photograph, covered by a series of groin vaults between arches of the Franciscan church's type. I know nothing however, about the circumstances of its building.

THE FIRST GOAN CHURCH: SANTANA DE TALAULIM

In chronological terms, the first church in architectural history that merits being called a Goan church is that of Santana, at Talaulim, a Jesuit foundation of 1577, rebuilt between 1682 and 1689 under the supervision of the Goan priest Francisco do Rego (1638–89). Rego studied theology in Portugal and returned to Goa circa 1675 to become the parish priest of S. Brás, Ilhas. As we already know, he was a Brahmin. According to Barbosa Machado, he was also a poet of some merit in both Portuguese and Latin. Having lived in Lisbon in the early 1670s he had certainly witnessed the transformation then beginning to take place in Portuguese church architecture, especially in what concerns interior design. Between the 1670s and the early 1700s, Lisbon's church interiors were covered with wooden gold-gilt altars with solomonic columns, volutes, capricious angels and cherubs. The walls were panelled with blue and white tiles depicting Old and New Testament scenes. Cornices, column and altar bases were decorated with Italian-inspired multi-coloured inlaid marble work. At the time when Francisco do Rego was in Portugal these transformations were only at their beginning. However, a clear tendency for a voluminous type of architectural sculpture in church wooden altars was already dominant in Portugal since the mid-17th century and must have impressed

Santana de Talaulim, Goa, 1682–1689

the Goan priest. Furthermore, while in Europe, he could have travelled to Rome where he would have seen Roman baroque architecture in its full splendour.

The original church of Santana was built to serve as a recreation *quinta* for the novices of the S. Paulo college in Old Goa. The Jesuits chose Talaulim because this was an important location in the outskirts of Old Goa, dominated by some powerful Catholic-Brahmin families. Over time many mansions and houses of both Portuguese and Goan aristocrats were built at Talaulim and this explains the unusual dimensions of the building (it had to house hundreds of attendants to the mass). The fact that Goan Brahmin priests took over the church since the late 16th century could have resulted from the importance of Goan aristocracy at Talaulim itself. Talaulim became deserted in the course of the 18th and 19th centuries, the aristocratic mansions disappeared, and the powerful Goan families shifted their residences to other localities in Goa.

Santana is a great monument, not only because of its quality and size, but because it is the end result of the evolution of church architecture in Goa since the late 16th century in a new and highly original synthesis. In Santana we have the Jesuit semi-circular niches along the nave, the Goa Augustinian type of western façade, the new vaulting system of the 1650s, a completely new type of wall design, and a never-seen-before concept of moulding and ornament.

The church has a six-bay single nave with lateral semi-circular niches, a true transept as in Margão but wider and higher, and a three-bay deep chancel with a magnificent *camarin*

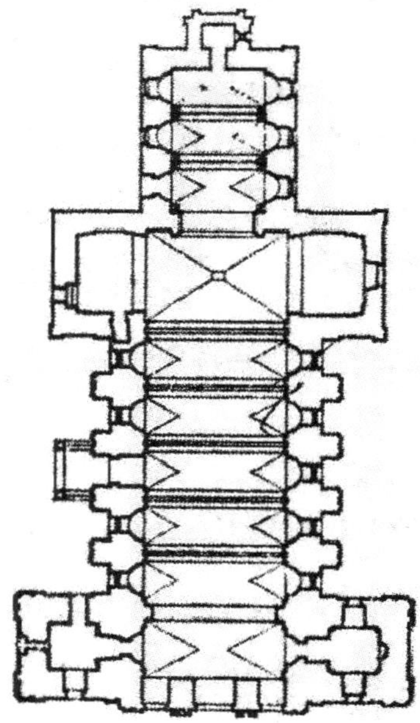

Santana de Talaulim, plan (drawing by M.T. Chicó)

Santana de Talaulim, chancel

and tabernacle. It is covered by six very narrow rectangular coffered planed barrel vaults with lateral penetrations between arches, again like Margão, which obviously was its architectural prototype. The crossing has a planed groin vault (a rectangle of normal dimensions) and the chancel is covered with a planed barrel vault with three penetrations and no dividing arches.

The walls of the nave have a gallery running over the lateral niches turning balconies toward the interior, a traditional Portuguese Jesuit theme that the Company had perhaps used in now disappeared Goan churches but not in any of those that have survived until today, although we do see it in Diu's Jesuit church of the early 17th century. This theme was also put in practice by the Franciscans at Old Goa's Espírito Santo and by the Theatines at Divina Providência and it could have been from there that Santana's architect got his idea.

The second gallery or clerestory, running above the first, and connecting the openings and windows between the penetrations is an original creation. Two superimposed galleries thus excavate Santana's walls with views to both the inside and the exterior of the church, acting like superb belvederes over the surrounding paddy fields, hillocks and coconut groves. The chancel and niches, the vaults, the interior elevations and the western façade are articulated and ornamented by architectural and decorative themes not previously used in such a systematic manner.

Santana de Talaulim, interior towards the chancel

Santana de Talaulim, north interior elevation, detail

Espírito Santo, Margão, interior order

Let us compare the nave elevations of Santana and Margão's Espírito Santo, because this is Santana's direct predecessor, the building from which padre Rego took inspiration for his plan, his vaults, his elevation design: In Talaulim the architect has introduced an intermediary order between the niches and the clerestory in order to respond to the three-level organization of his wall (niches-gallery-clerestory). The lower system is the same as in Margão (niches between an order of pilasters), but its treatment is completely different in character: in Santana we see a nervous rhythm of narrower niches and filled up surfaces leaving practically no blank space, pilasters with double shafts covered with very wide composite flowery capitals, expressively ornamented mouldings in the arches. The frieze and entablature, on the other hand, remain Ionic and a direct quote of Margão's.

The upper order is a compression of the lower: again we see a system of double shafted pilasters of a composite-Ionic order separating openings. In Western architectural terms the pilasters have totally wrong proportions and the openings are tabernacle-like with pairs of pseudo-solomonic columns framing arches topped by pediments. It looks like a sculpturally intense sum of architectural fragments.

Santana de Talaulim, lower order

Santana de Talaulim, façade, drawing by M. T. Chicó, pub. Azevedo 1969

Santana's main façade does not refer to Margão but to the prestigious model of Nossa Senhora da Graça, the structure of which is almost exactly reproduced. As for ornamental articulation, it effects the same change that it did for Margão's internal system: it renders it much more complex: pilasters are doubled and compressed, shafts gain fluting, surfaces are given ornaments of the Bom Jesus type but many times over, and topping motives are duplicated.

The Second Goan Church: Piedade de Divar

In a booklet published in 1902, the author, a native from the island of Divar named Cipriano da Cruz Gomes, claims that he heard from his grandmother, who in turn would have heard from her father deceased in 1851 that the Brahmin Goan priest António João de Frias (1664-1727), an ancestor of theirs, native from the village of Talaulim, was involved in the construction of the church of Santana when he became disappointed at the way the church was being built. He would have decided to outdo Santana's design when he became responsible for the parish of Divar and for the building of the new parish church of Piedade started in 1699, 10 years after the conclusion of Santana de Talaulim.

Whether this anecdote is true or the product of Cipriano da Cruz Gomes family's fantasies we don't know but the story of a rivalry between the designers of the two churches is interesting. Padre Frias became quite famous in Goa and in Portugal at the beginning of the 18th century for reasons other than architecture: he was the author of *Aureola dos Indios & Nobiliaria Bracmane*, a book that I mentioned in my introduction, published in Lisbon in 1702, which is a eulogy of the Brahmins in general and of the Catholic Brahmins in particular. We understand that Frias was a Brahmin—and so was Cipriano da Cruz Gomes and obviously his family as well—and a member of the Brahmin Goan clergy. His book dedicates important pages to the praise of the 'native' bishops of India.

In any case, be it true or the stuff of fantasy, Cipriano da Cruz Gomes' story makes it somewhat mandatory for us to discuss the architecture of Nossa Senhora da Piedade at Divar by comparing it with Santana de Talaulim, although we may recall that father Francisco do Rego, the likely designer of Santana, was also a Brahmin and also an author of a book in favour of the Brahmins, which, contrary to Frias, he never managed to publish. The comparison should not deter anyone from enjoying Piedade for its own merits: it is a truly outstanding building, one of the more beautiful churches of Goa, and if ever the word Baroque is to be applied with propriety to an Indian building than let this be the one.

Piedade's plan is different from Santana's. Padre Frias—I will assume that he was indeed the architect—chose a prestigious European architectural *parti* that had only very seldom been used in Goa: the church with inter-communicating lateral chapels that I have already discussed when we encountered its first Goan cases, which were the lateral chapels of the Cathedral and the Augustinian church of Nossa Senhora da Graça. I am persuaded that this *parti* was chosen for Divar not only because of the prestige of the precedents but because padre Frias had meditated about the buttressing system put in practice at the Cathedral where, I recall, the adding of the lateral chapels to the three naves permitted a pyramid-like discharge of the vault's weight. With lateral chapels, which are wider than simple niches, the separating walls act as effective buttresses for the central nave's vault.

Also, differently from Talaulim, padre Frias dispensed with the clerestory. Piedade has only one gallery running over the lateral chapels. This allowed for the gain of a lot of space in height and Frias could put in place lofty galleries that really look like palatial loggias with elegant arches.

But there were other, and perhaps more substantial, advantages to this change of architectural *parti*. What he dispensed with in height, the architect made up for in breath: the church's nave is wide like a hall, not high and narrow like a tunnel as is the case of Talaulim.

The vaulting system goes back to the Franciscans in Old Goa, not the Jesuits in Margão: at Divar, the nave is covered by five planed square groin vaults between arches, the crossing by one square planed groin vault, and two planed groin vaults cover the chancel. The arches

N.S. da Piedade, Divar, view of the gallery

N.S. da Piedade, Divar, interior towards the altar

N.S. da Piedade, Divar, façade

come low on the nave's space enhancing its breath. A broad, palace-like, softly illuminated and lavishly decorated church: this is Piedade de Divar.

The width of the lateral chapels and of the galleries running above them allowed padre Frias to disguise the lateral buttressing structure of the church inside a box-like building of the traditional type: along the sides all one can see is a two-storey church with windows topped by triangular pediments. The *camarin*, a box-like chamber placed against the chancel's eastern outer wall, illuminates de tabernacle from behind even in the afternoon, making it glow against the soft light that bathes the interior of the church.

The nave of Piedade is more flowery than Talaulim and even more sculpturesque. Padre Frias chose the pseudo-solomonic column as the architectural member for the the lower and the upper order, together with composite capitals with elongated palm leaves and the traditional Ionic frieze and cornice. The west façade is a replica of Margão's type with the order and the ornaments used in the interior.

4

Churches of Salcete, Bardez and Ilhas, 17th and 18th Centuries

Bardez and Salcete

It would be interesting at this point to examine how the parish churches of Salcete and Bardez, built by Jesuits and Franciscans since the late 16th century, were reshaped in the 18th century in order to look more like the new churches that had appeared in Old Goa and Ilhas in the second half of the 17th century. After its invention at Talaulim and Divar, the Goan church type continued to evolve through the 18th century. The majority of the churches of Goa were completed or altered then and the new trend influenced the patrons and parishioners of existing churches when a new chancel or façade was added, as well as when a new church was built.

There is a very important common factor to the churches partially modified and to those built anew: many were commissioned by the village *comunidades* or by gaunkars, not by the regular clergy. This means that the buildings were thought out and built by Goans.

But before discussing the churches that were modified or built anew, I will describe the general panorama of religious architecture in Bardez and Salcete at the beginning of the 18th century. The churches of these two Goan regions evolved very differently in the 16th and 17th centuries and the differences between them did not disappear in the subsequent centuries.

Bardez and Salcete fell under the domain of the Portuguese crown in 1543. Parishes were created in 1552. Those of Bardez were put in charge of the Franciscans and the ones in Salcete were given to the Jesuits. At the end of the 16th century, there were in Bardez 11 Franciscan *Reitorias* or parish houses. The Franciscan frei Paulo da Trindade, writing circa 1635, refers to 17 and he enumerates them according to the way they would be seen by someone following the coast or sailing up the rivers; that is, the route by which people travelled at the time. Beginning at Reis Magos, the first Franciscan church, founded in 1555, his description leads us eastward to Britona's Our Lady of Penha de França (founded 1626). and, turning north along the Mandovi's tributary, to Salvador-do-Mundo or Sirulá (1565), Pomburpá (Bumburupá in his spelling, founded in 1590), Aldoná (1569), Ucassaim (1621), Moirá (1636) and Mapuçá (1594). Then frei Paulo goes back west, to near Reis Magos, where he resumes his course at Nerul (1569) and continues to Candolim (1560), Calangute (1595), Nagoá (1560) and Guirim (1604), thus returning to very near Mapuça. His third tour starts on the ocean shore at Anjuna (1603) and goes inland along the Chaporá valley: Siolim (1600), Colvale (1591), Tivim (1623).

At practically the same time, Pedro Barreto de Resende completed his panoramic drawing of Bardez for the report of António Bocarro: he shows exactly 17 churches. Today there are many more parish churches in Bardez, of course.

Although Bardez and Salcete churches follow the same type (all are roofed single nave churches with a vaulted chancel and no lateral chapels), the façades are easily distinguishable and the built complexes that integrate the churches are also completely different in both talukas. Several church complexes of Bardez maintain the old *Reitoria* typology: to one of the sides of the church there is a cloister, often small and sometimes two-storey-high; a roofed portico protects its four galleries and gives access to the residence of the priests, the lateral door to the church, a wooden stair to the choir over the church's entrance, the parish school and other parish programmes. The whole complex looks like a little secluded convent. Buildings like this still exist in good condition at Salvador-do-Mundo, Parrá, Nagoá, Calangute, Candolim and other places. The type is so evocative and formally strong that the church of Saligão was modelled on these lines in the mid 19th century, long after the Franciscans had disappeared from Bardez.

These *Reitorias* strongly differ from the Salcete church complexes. Here there are no cloisters. The parish buildings are located to one side of the church with which they are connected via a porticoed lateral gallery. Sometimes (at Carmoná and Betalbatim, for instance) the church and the parish building form a U-shaped complex, and the patio thus created is enclosed by a wall with a gate, architecturally highlighted by a pediment or some other distinctive element. This is because the Jesuits were not a conventual order and their parishes in Salcete did not have to adopt a convent type. However, there is one exceptional Jesuit structure in Salcete: Verná. Along with the church, built in 1612, a Jesuit college-like building of the same epoch has survived until the present. The church occupies the east side of the built quadrangle, the façade turned north, aligned with the 'college' main façade. This building maintains a well-preserved cloister, but it seems to have resulted from different construction phases. It is not clear why the Jesuits have built this type of structure at Verná.

Verná, church and church building, begun 1612

Salcete was divided into 59 parishes in 1552 but its politico-military control was by no means secured until the beginning of the 1580s due to a state of permanent war with the Bijapuris who constantly raided the territory. Therefore, the first churches, made of lath and plaster and covered with *olas*, were built only in the fortification of Rachol and at the more important settlements or at sites where the first conversions took place: Cortalim (where the Zuari river was crossed between Ilhas and Salcete), the fort of Mormugão, the locations of Margão, Orlim and Verná.

The map of the mouth of Goa drawn by Manuel Godinho de Eredia in 1610 identifies 13 locations dotted with churches in Salcete and Mormugão, besides Rachol and Chandor (where there was no church at the time): Margão, Orlim, Carmoná, Benaulim, Cansaulim, Assolná, Chinchinim, Curtorim, Loutolim (Eredia writes Noutolim), Verná, Cortalim, Sancoale and Mormugão (Santo André).

Pedro Barreto de Resende locates 22 churches in his map drawn circa 1635 and the list compiled by Gomes Catão after Jesuit chronicles shows that 22 churches had been founded until that year in Salcete and Mormugão, plus three within the walls of Rachol: in alphabetical order, Assolná (1616), Benaulim (1596), Betalbatim (1630), Cansaulim (1588), Carmoná (1607), Chicalim (1625), Chinchinim (1590), Colvá (1630), Cortalim (1560),

Cuncolim (1604), Curtorim (1597), Loutolim (1581), Majordá (maybe 1588), Margão (1564), Mormugão (1570), Navelim (1597), Orlim (1568), Sancoale (1606), Seraulim (1630), Varcá (1635), Velção (1634), Verná (1568).

Franciscan Façades

Originally Franciscan and Jesuit church façades had no towers. These only appeared later. The first church by a religious order to sport towers in Goa was the Augustinian's N. S. da Graça, as we already know. And only after the example of Graça, that is, after the first quarter of the 17th century, did it occur to patrons throughout Salcete and Bardez that churches that were not Cathedrals could have towers The early Franciscan churches in Bardez had simple façades with three doors of the same size, sometimes protected by an exterior galilee. These façades still exist in practically all of the Bardez churches. The central three doors remained as a key feature when in the 17th, 18th and 19th centuries, two towers and two extra side bays were added, forming a five-bay façade.

The first Franciscan church in Bardez was Reis Magos, founded in 1555 on an eastbound slope of the Mandovi bank across from what is now the Campal and Miramar, in the immediate outskirts of Panjim. The church was built under the protection of the cannons of a fort,

Reis Magos, Bardez, Goa, façade after 1771

subsequently named Reis Magos after the church. The existing building is to a large extent the result of works conducted after 1771 (Catão 1955: 186). Comprehensive changes were then introduced to the church, so much so that even the Franciscan façade type was abandoned in favour of a simplified version of the five-bay-wide, four-orders-high Old Goa Augustinian type. Contrary to what happens in other Bardez churches with five bay façades, the three central doors are not distinguished from the others. The main door is larger, that is all.

The Reis Magos Franciscan complex played a very important role in the political geography of Goa because the Viceroys stayed there after arriving from Europe as they waited for their ceremonial entry into the city of Goa. The church was also the burial site of several Viceroys. A catechism school and an orphan's seminary functioned at times at the Reis Magos convent.

In the 1630s, Pedro Barreto de Resende included a very peculiar image of the building in his panorama of Bardez. We distinguish Reis Magos at the side of the powerful fort to which Resende gave due prominence. The overall disposition of church and convent can still be recognized in today's building: it is set against the steep slope of the hill, the cloister and the convent building to the north of the church. However, the church is shown with no towers at the façade but two at the rear, flanking the chancel, a very rare disposition that could have existed in the early 16th century at the Franciscan 'mother' church in Old Goa, Espírito Santo, as we already know (I am aware of only one other 17th-century Indian example of this type of chevet, which has also disappeared; the Jesuit college church of Saint Anne, Bandra, Mumbai, demolished in the 19th century and known only through a drawing).

Representation of Reis Magos fort and Franciscan convent and church, Pedro Barreto de Resende, ca. 1635

Reis Magos, Bardez, Goa, view of the church and Reitoria from the fort

Mãe de Deus, Pomburpa, Bardez, Goa, façade and staircase 18th century

Mãe de Deus, Pomburpa, Bardez, Goa, a) exterior view of the chevet b) interior view of the chevet

Furthermore, Barreto de Resende depicted a frontal staircase completely different from the straight and broad one that exists today: in the drawing we see an L-shaped staircase with a chapel or grotto built below it.

Amazingly, Barreto de Resende's image does indeed correspond to an existing building: the church and *Reitoria* of Mãe de Deus (Mother of God) in Pomburpa, a couple of kilometres to the east of Reis Magos. Every element is there: the L-shaped staircase negotiating the steep slope that separates the church from the road at the river bank, the presence of chambers below the staircase, the church placed against the hill facing east, two towers framing the chancel, the convent building standing on arches to the north on the hillside. Mãe de Deus was founded in 1590 but it is recorded that the staircase and two cells under it were built later. The mouldings and detailing of the existing façade, the chancel and the towers are from the second half of the 18th century.

We are therefore faced with two hypotheses: either Barreto de Resende depicted Pomburpa at the Reis Magos' site by mistake, and Pomburpa already had by then, in the 1630s, the overall form it presents today, or this form was given to Pomburpa in the 18th century as a memento of the old appearance of Reis Magos when the latter was completely transformed after the 1770s.

Salvador-do-Mundo, founded 1565, upper part of the façade: 18th and 19th centuries

The interior of Pomburpa's main chapel is clearly an 18th-century work. In fact, it is unique among all Goan churches because it presents itself as a paraphrase of the chancel of the Royal Basilica of Mafra in Portugal, a Franciscan monument completed in the 1730s under a prestigious commission by king D. João V: two superimposed galleries run along the perimeter of the chevet opening elegant balconies to its centre. A giant order of composite pilasters articulates the elevations and supports a penetration vault that reminds us of Mafra and, at the same time, of the Theatine's Divina Providência.

The basic Franciscan three-door façade has survived in the church of Salvador do Mundo. It was founded in 1565 but, again, we don't know what has remained of the original building. The body of the nave and the barrel-vaulted chancel, the false transept arches, the upper choir's supporting arch, all are decorated by simple mouldings that could be dated to the early 17th century. The façade, however, is clearly a later addition with its polygonal towers inspired by the Franciscan church in Old Goa (the central bell tower was probably added in the 19th century paraphrasing Panjim's parish church of Our Lady of Conception).

Facing the same eastern quadrant but a couple of kilometres to the south, the church of Penha de França displays a porch with staircase connected to a quay by the riverbank, the wide estuary of the Mandovi. The church was originally built by the Franciscans. It

Penha-de-França, after 1655, seen from the Mandovi river

Penha-de-França, façade

S. Francisco de Assis, Colvale, façade after 1713 and 19th century

S. Tomé, Aldona, founded 1596, façade and side-aisle 18th and 19th centuries

was extensivelly remodelled after 1655 (I will return to these works) and polygonal towers inspired by Old Goa were added, just as with the church in Salvador-do-Mundo.

Large five-bay towered façades like the ones of Aldona's S. Tomé (St. Thomas), Anjuna's S. Miguel (St. Michael), Colvale's S. Francisco de Assis, S. Diogo at Guirim, have all been totally or substantially rebuilt in the 19th century but they all maintained the Franciscan type. In the case of Aldona the left tower shelters the cloister gallery and the *Reitoria*'s doorway.

Jesuit Façades

The façades of the Jesuit churches first built in Salcete have not survived until the present day. All existing Salcete façades are from the 17th century or later. They fall into two models: the earlier façades were inspired by the Bom Jesus in Old Goa (built 1594–1605), the later by Margão's Espírito Santo (remodelled 1645). There is an exception, not in Salcete but in Mormugão (now Vasco), the façade of the Jesuit church of Santo André, founded in 1594, which was unfortunately demolished in the early 1950s to be replaced by a modern gothic structure. A published photograph of the old façade (Mascarenhas 2006: 105–12) shows a simple Franciscan-like composition enriched by a two-bay-deep, three-bay-wide portico or exo-narthex, similar to the one we can see at S. Miguel in Taleigão

Santo André, Mormugão, 1594-1628, façade demolished (photo published Mascarenhas 2006)

and also probably added later to the church. The church was remarkable for the fact that it had a single tower (still existing) located, also in the Franciscan manner, to the side of the chancel (one of the bells in this tower is dated 1628, which is probably when the church was finished).

The Bom Jesus type of façade was built at Loutolim (façade of uncertain date), Carmoná (1607), Verná (1612), Colvá (1635), Nuvem (1695), Majordá, Orlim, thus covering the whole of the 17th century. It was also built outside of Salcete at other churches, as for instance Santa Cruz in Ilhas, which was not a Jesuit church.

Differently from the Bom Jesus, the Salcete churches have one tower placed at the side but slightly withdrawn vis-a-vis the façade. The tower is located to the left at Loutolim, Carmoná, Colvá and Nuvem, to the right at Verná, eastwards at Santa Cruz. The seductive two-order tower at Orlim probably is a 19th- or early 20th-century alteration of an earlier structure. The exception is Majordá's Mãe de Deus: it has two towers placed behind the façade. Their upper order corresponds to an 18th-century campaign of works (1739). This campaign also changed the central part of the church façade, which looks very much like Colvá's, and replaced the vault over its chancel.

These withdrawn towers may be a typological trait inspired from single-tower west fronts of the type that I have discussed earlier in this book (let us recall Assolna, in Salcete, a Jesuit church with a peaked gable façade together with the lateral tower).

The façades of this group of churches have the form of narrow high rectangles, are three-bay wide, two-orders high (or three in the case of Verná), and are topped by a central fourth order under a pediment. The central section is connected to the lower lateral ones by scrolls

Salvador-do-Mundo, Loutolim, 1586, façade changed later

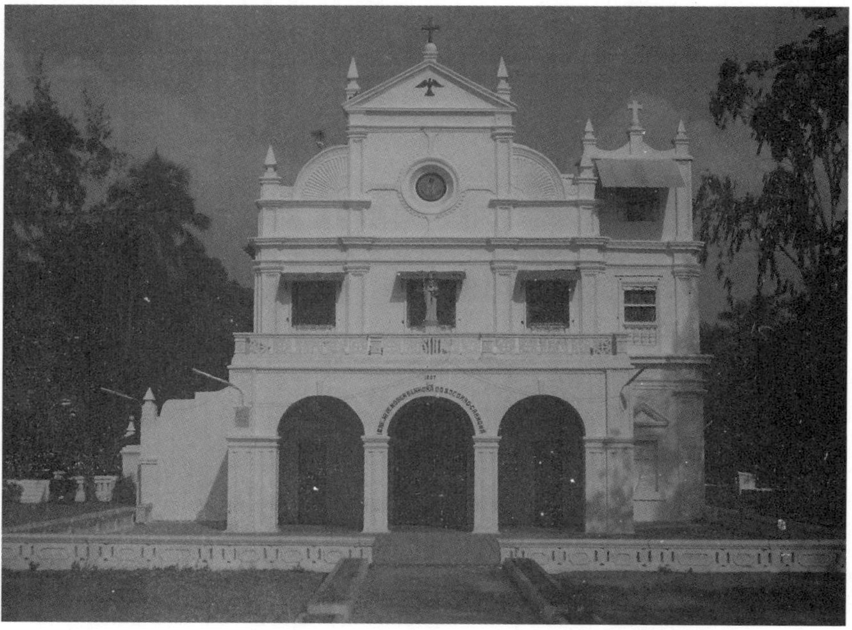

N.S. do Socorro, Carmoná, 1607, porch added in the early 1930s

Santa Cruz, Verná, 1612

N.S.das Mercês, Colvá, 1635

Mãe dos Pobres, Nuvem, 1695

Mãe de Deus, Majordá, founded 1588, façade altered 1739

S. Miguel, Arcanjo, Orlim, founded 1568, façade late 16th and 19th centuries

Santa Cruz, rebuilt 1710

that normally take the Bom Jesus type (these scrolls would be repeated or paraphrased in other Goan churches, in Salcete and other districts, throughout the 17th and the 18th centuries: Talaulim, Navelim, Benaulim, Chicalim, Cortalim, Varcá, Pilerne).

The strangest façade of the whole series is Loutolim's. The church, dedicated to Christ the Saviour, was begun in 1581, but the façade was obviously done later, the upper part of it being almost certainly from a much, much later time, probably the 19th or even 20th century: the central oculus, the scrolls, and the central templet are of an eclectic style very different from the rest of the composition. The Flemish type of decoration of the second order and the profusion of columns also represent a bit of an overstatement (see in contrast the decoration of the façades of Verná or Colvá).

One should also perhaps consider the west front of the church of Cortalim within this series. Nothing else remains of the building except the façade and tower, the rest having been destroyed and replaced by a modern construction in the first half of the 20th century. The original church, founded in 1566, was the Jesuits' first in Salcete and it has therefore been the object of a great deal of literature, unfortunately and as usual, very vague in historical terms. However, and for once, we know the name of the architect of the church, the Jesuit Francisco Aranha, a Spaniard or a Portuguese (the sources disagree) who would shortly after

Salvador-do-Mundo, Loutolim, detail of façade

S. Filipe e S. Tiago, Cortalim, façade late 16th century

become one of the martyrs of Cuncolim. The existing façade is not by him because, like the other façades in this series, it was built in the late 16th or early 17th century. Its model was not the Bom Jesus but the Sé Cathedral, of which it carefully paraphrases the central three-bay articulation and the topping elements. It is obvious that it was supposed to have two towers (only the western one was begun) and these would also have been like the ones at Old Goa both in their form and in their articulation with the central part of the façade.

The origin of the Margão church type of west front is the church of the Augustinians in Old Goa: a façade with a three-bay-wide, three-order-high central part, which is slightly foregrounded vis-à-vis lateral towers of two, three or four orders (in Salcete they never reached five orders like their Augustinian prototype). The simple crowning of the Augustinian church was replaced in the Salcete Jesuit buildings by multiple pediments, which were sometimes quite elaborate.

But in fact, a new form was added: the domes and lanterns crowning the towers. This became one of the more striking distinguishing traits of Goan 18th-century churches.

This type of tower crowning might have made its appearance for the first time at the Espírito Santo de Margão. As far as I am aware, the only towers crowned by domes that existed in Goa until then were those of the Theatine's Divina Providência. However, the form of these domes was too alien to Goan and Portuguese architectural habits: the Theatine towers are topped by pediments and the domes are conical, a rather odd interpretation of the Roman polygonal church tower domes of the late 16th century.

The inspiration for Goan tower domes and lanterns was, to my view, the mother church of the Augustinians in Lisbon, S.Vicente de Fora, built at the same time as its Goan counterpart as we already know. This is where the first towers crowned by domes appeared in Portuguese architecture. I think that Nossa Senhora da Graça in Old Goa also had domes and lanterns over the towers. They had already collapsed in the single surviving tower when the famous photograph by Sousa & Paul and other images were produced, and this is why no one has ever noticed them.

Margão's west front articulation directly inspired six very refined 18th-century alterations to existing façades in Salcete, along with a host of incomplete or half-hearted attempts at blending the Margão type with other types of façades. The five churches are, in alphabetical order, Benaulim, Betalbatim, Chinchinim, Curtorim, Sancoale and Varcá.

S. João Baptista, Benaulim, founded 1596, façade early 18th century

N.S. dos Remédios, Betalbatim, founded 1630, façade 18th century

N.S. da Esperança, Chinchinim, founded 1590, façade 18th century

Santo Aleixo, Curtorim, founded 1597, façade 18th century

The west front of Chinchinim is more massive, horizontally organized and ornamentally austere than the others. Benaulim and Varcá are very close to the prototype of Margão. In Curtorim's case the towers have gained a great degree of autonomy in relation to the central part of the façade thanks to very prominent drums, domes and lanterns.

The changing of the west fronts of churches to include the towers did not involve any modification in the interior of the nave. But the towers worked as frontal protection for exterior galleries running on one or two levels alongside the exterior walls, one of which is generally connected to the church's patio, as I have already pointed out. This happens more distinctively in Benaulim and Orlim (both have one gallery on the north side linked to parish buildings), Betalbatim (an arrangement of the same type but to the south and with a still existing patio doorway), Carmoná (with a fine patio and doorway) and at Varcá where one can see, and walk along, a very beautiful double gallery located on the church's northern flank.

The original church of Sancoale, Nossa Senhora da Saúde (Our Lady of Health), founded in 1606, was destroyed by fire in 1834. Only the central part of its 18th-century façade remains (it most likely had two towers). It quotes the façade of Benaulim's S. João Baptista (or was it vice-versa?) and it is one of the more beautiful in Salcete thanks to its splendid location facing east on the southern bank of the Zuari, and also because of its state of

S. João Baptista, Benaulim, side gallery

N.S. dos Remédios, Betalbatim, side galery

N.S. da Glória, Varcá, rebuilt after 1700

N.S.da Saúde, old church, Sancoale, 1606

preserved ruin (it has been a national monument since 1937) as well as the romantic isolation in which it stands.

Portuguese 18th-century Façades

There are very few façades in Goa that really look European or provide an aspect for which European stylistic terms are really appropriate. One of these is the main façade of the former Franciscan church of Mapuça, S. Jerónimo. The original building founded in 1594 is no longer recognizable. The church seems to have been remodelled in 1674 but it is very difficult to tell what changes were introduced then. All visible elements in the church seem to be the result of the intervention of Archbishop D. fr. Francisco de Assunção e Brito, sometime between 1775 and 1782, to which I have already referred in the previous chapter when writing about Franciscan *camarins*.

S. Jerónimo's façade is of this same period and it is a typical Portuguese second half of the 18th-century baroque façade. The three Franciscan bays and doors were kept and transformed into three vertical door-balcony-window sequences, a characteristic Italian baroque theme introduced to Portuguese architecture in the early 18th century. The façade is crowned by

S. Jerónimo, Mapuça, founded 1594, façade 1775–1782

a wide and high undulating pediment with scrolls and ovals, a rocaille cartouche, flaming pinnacles. The whitewashing gives it the final touch: one could easily be before a South Portugal parish church.

This façade was copied in almost every detail in the church of Santa Isabel de Portugal (St. Elizabeth of Portugal), Ucassaim, and the same type of crowning pediment appears at Tivim's São Cristovão (St. Christopher), at N.S. dos Milagres (Our Lady of Miracles), Sirsaim, at Santa Clara, Assonorá, at S. Francisco de Assis, Colvale, at S. Miguel, Anjuna, churches under the direct influence of Mapuça.

A variation of the model can be seen at the widely known chapel of Nossa Senhora da Piedade at Penelim, on the road to Old Goa. This façade was probably built around 1776, the year in which Rome conceded an Apostolic Brief to the chapel. Two pairs of finely carved pilasters frame the central door-balcony-window theme and support the undulating pediment. The perfection of the carving of the Composite order capitals and the fact that they are made of northern granite leads me to believe that they were appropriated from a demolished Old Goa building.

N.S. da Piedade, Penelim, façade ca. 1776

Remodelling of Chancels, Naves and Sacristies of Earlier Churches

Apart from the new façades, other modifications were introduced by church patrons to the buildings of Ilhas, Bardez and Salcete in the late 17th and in the course of the 18th century in order to make them appear more like *Divina Providência*, the sacristy of the Bom Jesus, the Franciscan's Espírito Santo; in one word: the new buildings of the Old City. Sometimes changes were confined to the nobler part of the church, the chancel. Richer or more determined patrons opted for the complete remodelling of their churches. Again, events seem to have occurred differently in Bardez and in Salcete.

For reasons that historians of things economic, social and religious could perhaps explain in the future, *comunidades* and gaunkars from Bardez seem to have been either wealthier, bolder or more independent than the church patrons of Salcete in their architectural commissions because only in Bardez do we find some cases of complete stone vaulting of churches (and not just the chancel), which was an expensive and hazardous building enterprise: three cases to be exact (and if I am not mistaken): the churches of Penha de França, Parrá and Colvale.

Penha de França is one of the better located churches in the vicinity of the old capital. Its façade is turned to the rising sun and the vast expanse of the Mandovi waters just before

N.S. da Penha de França, vault

the river is narrowed by steep margins as it passes in front of Panjim and meets the sea. The church stands right by the river waters from where it was accessible in the past via a stone quay under the façade's narthex. The first building was erected here in 1626 but the stone construction only took place after 1655. Judging by the architectural mouldings and the altars, the church was fully completed only in the early 18th century: this is when the barrel vault with penetrations covering the nave and the false transept were built, as well as the groin vault over the chancel, the façade, and even the simple but elegant pilasters, pediments and the door of the lateral northern façade facing the *terreiro*, which disguises, behind its palazzo-like design, the buttressing system of the vault.

The church of Santana at Parrá is much smaller and simpler. It faces, not the waters of the Mandovi but a large *terreiro* beyond which lies an even larger expanse of paddy fields. It was founded in 1649 but, as it was partially destroyed as a consequence of a Maratha incursion, the local gaunkars have built it anew in 1688. I believe that this is when the nave was vaulted. The nave pilasters, the cornice and the false transept are earlier than the barrel vaults with penetrations built between arches that cover nave and chancel, which could mean that only the roof and the chancel's vault of the original church would have disappeared in the

N.S. da Penha de França, north façade

Santana, Parrá, rebuilt 1688 (photo Joaquim R. dos Santos)

Santana, Parrá, detail of false transept and vault

Maratha attack. Strong buttresses were built against the southern exterior wall to support the vault. The cloister gallery to the north is covered with groin vaults that behave as buttresses on that side.

Twenty odd years later, in 1713, a third Bardez church was fully vaulted by the local gaunkars: Colvale. It has the simplest barrel vault with penetrations of the three but, like Parrá, it exhibits the powerful buttresses, which were necessary to support the vault. The former *Reitoria* building was located behind the church's chancel, taking full advantage of the spectacular position of the building on the southern bank of the Chaporá river.

Other remodelling operations in Bardez churches limited themselves to the covering anew of the chancels with penetration vaults. This is what must have happened for instance at the church of Nagoá, one of the earlier Franciscan foundations in Bardez, dated 1560. It was rebuilt after 1679. The façade, tower and all internal mouldings look early 17th century. The chancel's vault probably corresponds to the later campaign.

At Pilerne's S. João Baptista, the original small chapel built in 1658 was transformed into a full-fledged church later in the century and gained its present appearance probably in the mid-18th century with the building of the façade (a quotation of the Reis Magos present façade) and of the groin vault that covers the chancel.

S. Francisco de Assis, Colvale, 1713, detail of the interior

Santíssima Trindade, Nagoá, rebuilt 1679, interior

S. João Baptista, Pilerne, detail of the chancel's vault

The largest church in Bardez is N.S. da Esperança (Our Lady of Hope) at Candolim. It was a Franciscan foundation like many others until it was refounded and rebuilt by the *comunidade*. This took place in 1667 and subsequent years. A hundred years later in 1764, the two very high towers (the highest in any parish church in Goa) that attract attention to the building from across paddy fields and riverbanks were built. The nave is very wide but simple, a box covered with a roof. The chancel is covered by a bi-partite groin vault, today partially obstructed by an altar, which is too large for the chancel.

In Salcete, changes were often limited to the chancel where the Jesuit "invention" of the semi-circular niches with shell-like domes was introduced together with penetration vaults.

One can see a good example of this in the Jesuit church of Nossa Senhora da Esperança at Chinchinim, a roof covered, single nave church with a false transept, which was given a new chancel sometime in the 18th century: a barrel vault with lateral penetrations covers it and two semi-circular niches per side animate its elevations.

The new chancel of Majordá's church is dated with reasonable certainty: the church was burned in a Maratha incursion of 1738 and was rebuilt immediately after. The chancel is deep, covered with a barrel vault with penetrations and articulated by three semi-circular niches on each side.

N.S. da Esperança, Candolim, rebuilt 1667, towers 1764

N.S. da Esperança, Chinchinim, view of the chancel

Mãe de Deus, Majordá, view of the chancel

Chancels of the exact same type can be seen at Verná, Carmoná and Benaulim and, with penetration vaults but without niches, at Betalbatim, Querim and other Salcete churches.

Groin and not barrel vaults with lateral penetrations were preferred in other churches. A good example is Pangim's parish temple of Nossa Senhora da Conceição (Our Lady of Conception) founded in 1619. Of the original building, only the structure of the church's four walls, the triumphal arch, the transept arches and a chapel opening to the right arm of the transept have remained untouched until today. The façade and the chancel are from the 18th century (with the exception of the belfry, which is modern). The chancel is covered by a bi-partite groin vault and has two shell-shaped semi-circular niches per side.

The small chapel of N.S. de Todo-o-Bem (Our Lady of Todo-o-Bem) at Verem, built before 1726 (Catão 1955: 186), displays the only case known to me in early 18th-century

N.S. da Conceição, Pangim, founded 1619, façade 18th and 19th centuries

N.S. da Conceição, Pangim, view of the chancel

Chapel of N.S. de Todo-o-Bem, Verem, before 1726, interior towards the chancel

Bardez of a nave articulated by semi-circular niches. Futhermore, the building, a little jewel of careful proportioning, detailing and ornamentation, also sports a groin vault with penetrations covering its chancel, and elderly local parishioners remember that a similar vault existed over the nave, having been demolished because it was threatening to collapse. It has the appearance of a little Jesuit Margão-like church that would have been built north of the Mandovi.

In Salcete, penetration vaults and semi-circular niches were standard solutions in the 18th century: at Benaulim's S. João Baptista, the remodelling that took place in the 18th century resulted, apart from the new chancel, in a highly decorative façade and in a new sacristy bearing all the signs of novelty: it is a rectangular room, fairly low, covered by a wide groin vault with lateral penetrations decorated with stucco coffers and divided into three bays. To these bays correspond, on the lateral walls, six niches with shell shaped semi-domes.

The church of Santa Cruz, Ilhas, was extensively rebuilt in 1710. The façade (which is of the Bom Jesus type with one tower slightly withdrawn), and the chancel covered with a

S. João Baptista, Benaulim, sacristy, first half of the 18th century, detail

Santa Cruz, sacristy, after 1710, detail

barrel vault with penetrations, must correspond to this campaign of works. But its piece-de-resistance is the sacristy, in particular due to the rich stuccowork that covers the bi-partite groin vault with penetrations and the tabernacle-like doors and niches.

What was also extraordinary was that church patrons in Ilhas changed their minds about the type of building they wanted once construction was well under way. The church at Curca was founded in 1646 according to most common sources or in 1668, according to the *Cronista de Tissuary* (II: 176) quoted by Ricardo Telles (1940–41: 277). But the first mass was celebrated only in 1690, this being the date when the works were concluded (Rocha 1973: 444). The chancel is covered by a traditional coffered barrel vault. The frontal and northern lateral façades belong to the type of austere architecture inspired by Old Goa's Júlio Simão cycle. Sometime in mid-course a different design must have been chosen because the nave of Rosário is almost a replica, to scale, of Margão's Espírito Santo: it has the same type of semi-circular niches along the sides, the same kind of pilastered order. The vault is also similar, only slightly planed. In the arches of the false transept one can clearly see how a previous articulation was replaced by a new order and by niches inspired by the example of Margão. It seems that when the patrons chose to have the nave fully vaulted, they opted for a Margão-style type of interior, abandoning the traditional articulation used in the chancel.

N.S. do Rosário, Curca, concl. 1690, lateral façade

N.S. do Rosário, Curca, detail of the interior

N.S. do Rosário, Curca, detail of the false transept

The New Churches of the 18th and early 19th Centuries and Cupoliform Façades

Besides having a new vault built over their church chancels or partially rebuilding the elevations of their naves, Goan 18th-century church patrons resorted to a third option: to build new churches. These were single-nave buildings almost without exception covered by roofs, the chancels covered by groin vaults with penetrations. They had semi-circular niches running along the sides of the nave on one or two storeys. The façades were flanked by towers.

The church of Chandor, founded in 1645, has niches along the walls of the nave but not in the chancel, contrary to what one would expect. This is covered by a groin vault which forced the builders to display on its exterior a crown of supporting buttresses (the church definitely had construction problems: its façade collapsed in 1949 and was replaced by a modern gothicizing affair, which is not really very successful).

Nossa Senhora do Rosário (Our Lady of the Rosary) of Navelim, a Jesuit church founded in 1597 and rebuilt after 1739 is very eclectic: its nave's lateral niches seem to have been inspired by the Bom Jesus sacristy: they are polygonal in plan instead of semi-circular.

N.S. de Belém, Candor, begun 1645, view of the chancel

Polygonal arches cover the windows of the gallery that runs over these niches on the church's second storey, articulated by a short and wide pilaster order. The Bom Jesus example is also visible in the chancel's barrel vault with penetrations: these have a stucco fan design like the Jesuit sacristy's vault. The frontal façade, on the contrary, directly quotes the polygonal towers of the Franciscan's convent church façade in Old Goa although it also makes use of Jesuit-like scrolls and pediment.

Two other churches are much more coherent than these: they are located outside Salcete and Bardez: Mandur, Ilhas, a private foundation of 1710 by a gaunkar, and S. Francisco Xavier, Chicalim, in the area of Mormugão, rebuilt by the local *comunidade* in 1747. They are both truly remarkable buildings.

The church of Nossa Senhora do Amparo (Our Lady of Refuge) in Mandur has the most striking façade of all Goan churches, with two very plain and classical four-order towers with, in between them, a four-order-high central section that is not plain and not classical, to say the least: it displays solomonic columns, round-headed windows, an oculus, a sculpturally dense templet with the image of Our Lady, the whole composition topped by the crowning eagle wings of the arms of the Augustinian order like spikes raised up in the sky. This is flanked by scrolls and volutes like we can see nowhere else in Goa or, for that matter, in the world.

N.S. do Rosário, Navelim, rebuilt after 1739, detail of the interior

N.S. do Rosário, Navelim, view of chancel's vault

N.S. do Amparo, Mandur, beg. 1710 (photo David M. Kowal)

The festival of adventurous forms continues inside: the church has a single-roof-covered-nave and a chancel covered by a groin vault, but all the rest is unusual: the niches that articulate both chancel and nave (on two levels) have the shape of doors and windows of a very shallow semi-circular curvature covered with shell-shaped crownings. Superimposed pilasters decorated like filigree separate niches along the walls. Extraordinary stucco relief inspired by the art of bed-quilts or porcelain cover all surfaces.

In the case of Chicalim's S. Francisco Xavier, the interior's lower order is a replica of Santana de Talaulim to a much reduced scale: minutely decorated niches between double shafted Corinthian (palm-leaved) pilasters. The upper storey repeats the pilaster order, now articulating simple rectangular verandas to the exterior. Over the chancel, with niches and pilasters of the nave type, we can see a barrel vault with penetrations. Just like in Mandur, festive stucco-work covers all available surfaces. The façade remained incomplete, one of the towers never having been built: the central section is a variation upon Mandur's themes. The existing tower displays a polygonal drum like Salcete's churches, but with no cupola.

N.S. do Amparo, Mandur, view towards the altar (photo Joaquim R. dos Santos)

N.S. do Amparo, Mandur, chancel's vault (photo Joaquim R. dos Santos)

S. Francisco Xavier, Chicalim, 1747, detail of order (photo Joaquim R. dos Santos)

S. Francisco Xavier, Chicalim

The more interesting new Goan 18th-century churches have a specific type of west front characterized by the presence between the two towers of a half-cupola with drum, dome and lantern serving no purpose except to give the illusion of the existence of a complete cupola to onlookers standing in front of the church. José Pereira designated this type of façade as 'cupoliform' in 1995 and they were discussed for the first time in Portuguese architectural history by José Manuel Fernandes in 1998–99.

The cupoliform-façade churches, a Goan 'invention' if ever there was one, constitute the climax of the evolution toward a characteristically Goan church that we have been following since Espírito Santo de Margão, Nossa Senhora da Piedade de Divar and Santana de Talaulim. This is particularly true of the most remarkable of the whole group because it was the first and also because it was the only fully vaulted cupoliform church: Santo Estevão (St. Stephen) of Juá, founded by the local *comunidade* in 1759.

Santo Estevão is isolated at the far end of the island of Juá, away from the village, facing the setting sun, the open sky, a vast extension of paddy fields, with Old Goa visible to the south, and Panjim in the horizon. It is, in a certain sense, the complete Goan church. It has

Santo Estevão, Juá, began 1759

Santo Estevao, Juá, interior toward the chancel

Santo Estevao, Juá, detail of the chancel

groin vaults between arches, the semi-circular niches of Margão and Talaulim articulating its chancel. The nave sports lateral chapels like Divar but, differently from Divar, they present no inter-communicating passages.

To all of these elements, the builders have added the cupoliform or false dome façade. Only from a certain distance does the false cupola work its wondrous illusion and make the façade recall the Theatine church in Old Goa with its dome between towers composing a Roman skyline. This was probably the intention of whoever invented this type of façade and of the patrons who accepted and paid for it: to have something different from the tradition, something more modern, something Italian. The false cupola solved the problem of the scarce frontal visibility of the dome in basilical-plan churches that Western architects always experienced with dismay and that the architect of the Theatines in Old Goa had not managed to solve: it brought the dome forward and placed it between the towers, albeit in a purely scenographic manner.

I would suggest that this 'invention' originated in Juá and not in the church normally described as the first of the type, Santo Aleixo (St. Alex), Calangute, a Franciscan foundation of the late 16th century built anew by the *comunidade* between 1741 and 1765. I would think that the architect and patrons of Santo Estevão should be credited with the novelty, first

Santo Estevão, Juá, detail of false dome and tower

Santo Aleixo, Calangute, 1741–1765, façade probably concluded later

because their building is larger, richer, fully vaulted, and second because it is located in Ilhas, a Goan region which has a characteristically autonomous architectural tradition as we already know and where most innovations in church design appeared.

What could have happened is that the Calangute *comunidade* decided to adopt Juá's novel type of west front when the construction of their church, Santo Aleixo, was under way, having started in 1741 at the chancel as was the habit of the times. One should take notice that the towers and the ornament (namely the pediments over the windows) in Calangute's façade seem to be much later in style than the 18th century. They are clearly 19th and even late 19th century, and similar to what we can see in the remaining cupoliform churches, but not in Juá, which is the only church in the series that seems to have been totally built in the 18th century.

The nave of the Calangute church is roof-covered and has semi-circular niches sheltering windows on two storeys. The chancel has an audacious groin vault but it was built in 1916 and I don't know what type of vault existed before, maybe the original late 16th-century barrel vault.

After Calangute another half a century had to go by before a local *comunidade* decided to experiment with the new type of west front: it happened at Moirá, again in Bardez. The local

Santo Aleixo, Calangute, detail of interior

N.S. da Conceição, Moirá, 1800–1836

N.S. da Conceição, Moirá, view from the west

N.S. da Conceição, Moirá, detail of façade

church of Nossa Senhora da Conceição was built by the *comunidade* for the Franciscans in 1636 but the west front and the chancel were completely rebuilt between 1800 and 1836, the façade probably continuing to undergo transformations until very late in the 19th century. The church was given a massive tower at the back of the chancel in 1836 following the model of Mapuça's S. Jerónimo, but not to crown a *camarin*, merely to support a heavy bell salvaged from the ruination of the Jesuit college of S. Roque in Old Goa. The façade was begun anew in 1800 in the cupoliform type. Its minutely carved orders, shell-like motives and eclectic ornaments are probably much later.

5

Epilogue

Modern Architecture and the Goan Church

The architectural and artistic treatise writers of Europe during the second half of the 15th century and of the 16th century, men like Alberti, Filarete, Serlio, Vasari, Delorme, proclaimed that the architecture of their times, Renaissance architecture, represented a complete break with the preceding type of architecture, the one that we know today as Medieval or Gothic.

This was not the first time in the history of the arts that novelty was hailed as a value per se or as a goal to be achieved. But these were certainly the first artists, patrons, theoreticians of the arts to have believed that they represented a new dawn in history—although they dressed the novelty of their endeavours in the trappings of the Antique, the arts of the Greco-Roman world of one thousand years before.

Renaissance artists were in consequence the first modern artists: they consciously sought a break with tradition, they deliberately proposed forms and looked for inspiration in sources that the common perception would not recognize; their culture was expressed and it spread through media, namely print, and through languages which were to a large extent alien to the dominant culture of their times.

Once established, Renaissance art and architecture never stopped changing, not only because of the different artists or artisans who practised it, or because of the different geographical, social and economic conditions in which they operated, but because it was modern: it had within itself the propensity for invention, experimentation and novelty. We acknowledge these changes through stylistic terms that are often too narrow to describe all the variety of styles and manners of art and architecture that flourished in Europe and the European-influenced world between 1500 and 1800: mannerism, baroque, rococo, neoclassical.

In spite of permanent change, a certain continuity was achieved in Western art and architecture throughout these three centuries, probably because very conservative forces—the church, the nobility—were at work employing artists and commissioning works of art and because economy and society were changing, albeit at a considerably slower pace than we have become accustomed to in more recent times. Decade after decade, people wanted the same type of church, of chapel, of house, of palace, the same kind of painting, of image. Forms of windows, for instance, could be altered under the pressure of novelty. New types of ornament could be tried out by excited patrons and eager architects. But the overall proportion, form and roofline of the façade where the windows and the ornament were to appear remained the same, its construction materials and techniques did not change.

Neo-gothic made its appearance in the last decades of the 18th century and triumphed in many parts of the art world in the first half of the 19th century. Again, with neo-gothic as with Renaissance three centuries before, novelty was proclaimed as the objective of the artist. Again, this novelty was described not as purely new but as a recovery of past values: this time, the same Gothic that Renaissance had discarded.

There was, however, a difference in historical circumstances. Unlike what had happened in the Renaissance, now, in the early 19th century, society itself, in the West and in the colonial world, with the industrial and the bourgeois revolutions, was at the beginning of an acceleration of pace never witnessed before in historical times, and the institutions that had granted to the arts a constancy of purpose for three centuries, the same church and nobility that had ruled Europe from the early Middle Ages, were now being put through a crisis that would terminate the historical significance of the aristocracy and severely threaten the importance of the church. In these revolutionary circumstances, changes in the arts could not be anything but revolutionary and this is what happened throughout the 19th century in Western art and architecture: constant turmoil, which would culminate, at the end of the century, with artistic avantgardes (the modernists) who, for the first time in the modern era, sought no historical precedent for their artistic propositions and set forward to look for the purely new.

Neo-gothic had been modern, as in the Renaissance, but not yet radically modern as with the modernists. When it was introduced, first as a kind of fashionable trend but later as a fiercely affirmative doctrine, with theoreticians and practictioners like Pugin, it came from within societies (the British, the French, the German) that had not forgotten the Middle Ages or its arts. In these societies neo-gothic did represent a link with the past, not a radical rupture.

But that was not so in British India and even less in Portuguese Goa. The history of the arts and architecture of the Iberian world is parallel to Europe's and is therefore unique in the context of the colonial world. In Goa or, say, Mexico, European art and architecture was introduced at the beginning of the Renaissance and underwent an evolution following the pattern of Western evolution (although, as we have seen in the case of Goa, soon becoming autonomous).

At the beginning of the 19th century, the architectural tradition of the Catholics of Goa was three centuries old. Neo-gothic, which was then becoming popular in cultivated circles throughout British India, was completely alien to this tradition. And it was also something else: it was foreign, it came from outside Catholic territories and from outside the Catholic world, originating in Evangelical architects and patrons.

Of course, in Britain, Augustus W. N. Pugin (1812–52), who had initiated neo-gothic as a doctrine, was a Catholic. He presented Gothic as a revival of true Chistian art against the 'paganism' of classicism. But I am not sure that the movement was perceived as primarily Christian by Goans. The sources I have been able to consult (19th century Goa and Bombay printing presses) indicate that the Goan elite admired neo-gothic churches and other buildings, namely the famous railway terminal and the government buildings of Bombay, because these were signs of monumentality, modernity and progress, not for religious reasons (V. Gomes 2007).

This leads me to conclude that neo-gothic architecture was the first modern architecture known to Goa. It represented a complete rupture with the past. It was perceived as standing for progress and modernity. To the eyes of Goan Catholics, it was purely new.

It was, therefore, not easily accepted. Its penetration was gradual, negotiated step by step. In the end, only a handful of neo-gothic churches were built and, more importantly, in the vast majority of cases, the style was reduced to superficial trappings: church builders adopted some gothic features (pointed windows being the prominent one) but kept to traditional church design principles.

The first neo-gothic church built in Goa was Madre de Deus (Mother of God) in Saligão, Bardez, built between 1867 and 1873. It was to remain the most remarkable one from the architectural point of view.

The church was designed by an architect (or engineer, there were no such differences at the time) of the *Departamento de Obras Públicas* (PWD) of the Government of Goa, Inspector Manuel Ferreira Martins, a man born in Goa of Portuguese descent in 1817 and who died in 1882 (I owe this information to the generosity of Alice Santiago Faria who is preparing an academic thesis on 19th- and early 20th-century architecture in Goa). The design was commissioned to him by the local *comunidade* through Francisco Salvador Zeferino Pinto, who was the President of the Municipality of Bardez and President of the Goan *Partido Progressista* (according to information provided by padre Nascimento Mascarenhas available on the Internet).

Alice Santiago Faria has drawn my attention to the fact that all neo-gothic Goan churches of the 19th and early 20th centuries, and all neo-gothic transformations of existing churches, took place in Bardez and in the area of Mormugão. For Alice Santiago Faria as well as for

Madre de Deus, Saligão, 1867–1873

myself, British influence is the only reasonable explanation for this fact. Mormugão was a hub of British economic and urban activity since the Anglo-Portuguese economic treaty of 1878, which determined the building of a railway between British India and the harbour of Mormugão. Bardez, on the other hand, was a region from where thousands of people migrated in the second half of the 19th century to Bombay, establishing in that city a number of burgeoning Goan colonies.

Migrant money and influence gave birth to Saligão's church—and the man who designed it, a *descendente* (the word used in Goa to refer to Goans with European or semi-European families) working for the PWD, certainly knew Bombay well as did all among the elite who ruled Goa, whether born in Goa or in Portugal (P.V. Gomes 2007).

The single tower façade of Madre de Deus shows the clear influence of the architecture of Bombay, namely the British-built Anglican cathedral of St. Thomas in the Fort, and so do the buttresses along the south façade, which are useless from the constructive point of view because a roof, not a vault, covers the church. The pinnacle supported by four concrete buttresses on the façade's tower constitutes the church's more rhetorical sign of 'gothicism'.

However, the gothic architecture of the Saligão church is also traditional to a certain extent: it is horizontal rather than vertical, whitewashed, and a Franciscan *Reitoria*-type

Madre de Deus, Saligão, view of the nave

of parish building was erected against its northern flank. The pointed arches along the southern façade have no correspondence in the interior where one can see traditional round arched windows. In spite of these traditional elements with Saligão, Goa had its first modern church.

Three decades after the Saligão church was concluded, Goan patrons commissioned another church that tried to look modern: Santo António (St. Anthony) of Siolim, again in Bardez, built between 1902 and 1907. This time, unlike what had happened in Saligão where no church existed, a previous 17th-century Franciscan structure was pulled down for the modern church to stand in its place. However, Siolim's church is typologically traditional, not gothic: all one has to do is to mentally replace all pointed arches with round arches or windows and the result is a perfectly 'normal' Goan single-nave church with a façade between towers.

The square classical porch with pointed arches, supporting an image of Cristo-Rei (Christ-the-King), was built against the main façade in 1931, a period during which the devotion to Christ-the-King triggered the construction of similar monuments all over Goa. The connection between the relative modernity of the church and Goan migrant communities in Bombay is made clear through an inscription, which one can see in the

Madre de Deus, Saligão, side view

Santo António, Siolim, 1902–1907

church patio, certifying that the altars of St. Anthony were paid for by the *sons of Siolim residing in British territory*.

Also at Siolim, the chapel of Mãe de Deus, designed and built between 1922 and 1927 at the site of the Franciscan's demolished original church, is a traditional building with gothic windows and doors (a bad photo of this church, wrongly identified with Saligão's Madre de Deus, was published in the Diocese *Memória* of 1933). Santo António, Vagator, concluded in 1925, a church inspired by Santo António of Siolim's example, is again of this very same type.

For many years, no other large gothic church was built in Goa. Several façades were modernized with the alteration of the design of windows and doors in favour of pointed arches; many altars and items of church furniture in wood were replaced by gothic-designed pieces, but it was only in the 1950s, when modern architecture arrived in Goa spearheaded by the last Portuguese Governors' wave of public works, that gothic-inspired church design resurface, now supported by concrete technology and disguised by abstract linear mouldings. This is the case of the new church of N.S. da Vitória (Our Lady of Victory) at Revorá, Bardez, built between 1946 and 1952 (which is interesting only because it sports a false gothic spire between two lateral towers thus recalling the Goan

S. José, Dramapur, 1848

cupoliform prototype), and the new façades of Chandor (1950) and S. André (St. Andrew) in Vasco (1953).

Gothic or neo-gothic was not, however, the only option available to Goan church patrons who wanted their buildings to appear modern in the 19th century: this could also be achieved with a neoclassical façade design. In the church of S. José (St. Joseph), Dramapur, a new parish in the heart of Salcete, built in 1848, we can see an interesting case of a neoclassicizing interpretation of Goan tradition: the façade is neoclassical, but the interior is purely Goan, a wide single-nave covered by a roof and a groin vaulted chancel, both ornamented with 18th century-type mouldings.

One of the first Goan churches to adopt a more decisive neoclassical appearance was the church of N.S. do Desterro (Our Lady of Exile) at Mormugão which father Nascimento Mascarenhas attributes to the design of the PWD engineer Randolfo Correia Mendes; it was built between 1884 and 1885 (Mascarenhas 2006: 131–32). According to Alice Santiago Faria, the engineer's complete name was Rodolfo Rosmiro (or Ramiro) Correia Mendes, also a Luso-descendent born in Goa in 1847 and who died in Lisbon in 1916. I am not certain that he was the designer of the Mormugão church because the same façade appears

Chapel of S. Sebastião, Fontainhas, Pangim, ca 1888

at the neighbourhood of Fontaínhas, Pangim, in the chapel of S. Sebastião (St. Sebastian), built between 1884 and 1888 during the regularization of the corresponding street by the experienced *Obras Públicas* engineer—soon to become its Vice-Director—João d'Assa Castelo-Branco (again, information I owe to Alice Faria).

The design is bold and effective: it does away with towers by locating a single bell in a niche placed at the top of the central part of the façade, powerful enough in its three-storey-high, one-bay-wide articulation to completely dominate the whole structure. A triangular pediment tops the portal and the composition is crowned by a curved one. Lateral rusticated sections, much lower than the centre, give the façade a wider base and shelter the accesses to lateral galleries.

The strangest of all architectural attempts at achieving a modern appearance in churches is the one that emerged when it was decided to pull down the old façade of the church of N.S. das Mercês (Our Lady of Merces), Ilhas, a typical late 16th- or early 17th-century church with its single roofed nave and its chancel covered with a barrel vault. The church had a narthex or porch added, of the type we can see at Taligão. What was built upon de porch (in the early 20th century?) was the only truly eclectic church façade existing in Goa. It almost succeeds in being at the same time neo-gothic (it has spires), neo-romanesque (see the

N.S. das Mercês, early 17th century, façade later

round windows), neo-manueline (observe the solomonic mouldings of the main window and of the niche), and, entirely original, exhibiting windows with frames in the form of the Portuguese Order of Christ's cross.

To me, the most significant of all late-modern Goan churches are not the half-hearted neo-gothic buildings or the neo-classical scattered cases but the churches which were deliberately built in continuity—one could even say in emulation—of the types of design that Goa had created in the 18th century. These churches fall into two types. The first is well represented by three buildings which were probably designed between 1860 and 1880: N.S. de Guadalupe (Our Lady of Guadalupe) in Batim, Ilhas, Santo André (St. Andrew), Goa-Velha, also Ilhas, and the church of Santana, Agonda, in Canacona, built by priests from Ilhas. An unwary observer, casually looking at their façades, would date them to the mid-18th century or even, in the case of Santo André, to the 1600s. The church of N.S. de Guadalupe in Batim was built between 1860 and 1867, replacing a 16th-century chapel. It is a single-nave church with a characteristic Goan Ilhas façade of the 1720s or 1730s. The central section reminds us of N.S. do Amparo at Mandur, for example. Only the pinnacles topping the lateral sections clearly show that it was a later design.

A second group of late 19th-century Goan churches is equally striking for its deliberate

N.S. de Guadalupe, Batim, 1860–1867

Santana, Bodiém, built 1893

continuity with 'Goaness'. In 1893, the small church of Santana built in 1801 for the new parish of Bodiém located to the west of Mapuça in a breathtakingly beautiful site facing horizon, fields and water, was completely rebuilt with a cupoliform type of façade, probably inspired by either Calangute or Moirá. The church has a nave and chancel articulated by niches and a penetration vault over the chancel, also like these precedents. The façade displays a simpler version of the type of ornament that we see at Moirá's Conceição.

Four years later, in 1897, another work of the same type and in the same region appeared with the completion of the reconstruction of the church of Assagão. The original chapel had been founded in 1775, affiliated to the parish church of Anjuna and dedicated to S. Caetano. The nave that resulted from the 19th-century reconstruction deserves mention for the richness of its niche-articulation in two levels inspired by the example of Calangute and the wooden barrel ceiling .

There is one lone cupoliform church (or rather a little chapel) that was built not in the whereabouts of Mapuça like all those we have described (Calangute, Moirá, Bodiém, Assagão), nor in Ilhas like the probable prototype of the series, Santo Estevão. This chapel is located deep in Salcete, on the outskirts of Loutolim. It is Nossa Senhora dos Milagres (Our Lady of Miracles) at Loutolim-Vanxém. The foundation date of the chapel, 1677, has been

S. Caetano, Assagão, church, cross and terreiro. Rebuilt 1894 (photo Joaquim R. dos Santos)

S. Caetano, Assagão, view towards the chancel (photo Joaquim R. dos Santos)

N.S. dos Milagres, Loutolim-Vanxém, façade probably late 19th century

established (F. Xavier de Araújo 1947), but it is obvious that the west front corresponds to a late 19th-century addition or transformation under the guidance of a patron who knew Santo Estevão or the new churches of Bardez.

In the last three decades of the 19th century and from then onwards to the early 20th century, church design reiterated and rearticulated the 'Goaness' of the Goan church, resolutely leaving aside any convinced or convincing attempt at modernity, precisely at the time when the domestic architecture of Goa attained its gloriously inventive climax and Goa was covered with beautiful residential buildings of all dimensions, from some large palatial mansions to many modest but impeccably designed houses, creating a panorama with few parallels in the history of architecture.

Judging from what has been published by cultural and social historians about Goa's cultural history in the 19th and early 20th centuries, especially in what concerns the problematic raised by Goan Catholic, Hindu and Portuguese elites in secular circles (see R. Pinto 2007), the conservative artistic development that we have witnessed seems somewhat unexpected. These circles have aspired to the modernization of Goa, albeit formulating this wish in different ways.

However, religious architecture forces historians to pay attention to other cultural actors in Goan 19th-century society: not the secular elite but the church. Not the politicians, the intellectuals or the litterateurs who aspired to progress, but our already familiar key cultural players in three centuries of Goan life: the Goan clergy. The 19th century as a whole, but particularly its second half, and even more specifically its last decades, was a time of turmoil within the Catholic church in India, a situation which affected Goan society's Catholic upper castes in a profound manner. I am of course referring to the issue of the Portuguese *Padroado* in its final confrontation with Rome's *Propaganda Fide*. Between the mid-19th century and the end of the 1920s, the secular institution of the *Padroado Régio* was put to rest. But it did not go quietly into the night. On the contrary. Especially in India, its defenders have put up a passionate fight for its survival.

It is worth noting, although it hardly ever was, that the institution of the *Padroado* was appropriated by the Goan clergy during the 18th century, so much so that in the 19th century the priests of Goa, and the upper caste society of Goa (and of Catholic Bombay), became the chief defenders of the *Padroado* against the Papacy, against *Propaganda*... and even against the Portuguese government in Europe and in India which tried to negotiate the slow demise of the *Padroado* with the Pope (C. Rivara 1858 and 1862; Hull 1927; Figueiredo 1939; Rego 1978).

Goans had taken due notice that they owed to the *Padroado* the appointment of their sons to parishes all over India and that, under *Propaganda*, European priests were taking over the churches of India. The *Padroado* had become an Indian institution (besides being a Goan one). On 21 October 1886, in the city of Panjim, a meeting took place, one of many in Goa, Bombay and other parts of India, to protest the new *Concordata* (agreement) between the Holy See and the Portuguese Government, which the land-owners, lawyers, doctors, businessmen, priests and other influential people of Goa believed to be detrimental to Catholicism in India (*Acta do Comicio*... 1886). The speeches, inflamed and pompous as these had to be considering the time and the place, exuded Goan pride: all speakers denounced *Propaganda* (and implicitly the Holy See) but also the Portuguese government, for discriminating against the Goan clergy. They all reminded Rome and Lisbon that no Goan had ever been appointed Archbishop of Goa in spite of the fact that Christianity in India owed a tremendous amount to Goans, including, it is explicitly stated, the building of churches paid for with Goan money. Defending the clergy of Goa, the prestige of Goan Catholic culture, the economic and social future of so many Goan families, became a question of life and death for Goan upper caste society.

It is therefore not surprising that some church patrons in Goa chose to build churches that appeared Goan, traditionally Goan, and not modern churches in the neo-gothic style, which could easily be identified with *Propaganda*. An architectural tradition in church design that was born in the 16th century and had become a Goan tradition at the end of the 17th century thus received a new lease of life in the late 19th century, lasting well into the 20th century.

Bibliography

Acta do Comício de 21 de Outubro de 1888 reunido em Nova Goa, Nova Goa, Typographia de 'Times of Goa', 1886.

ALBUQUERQUE, Teresa, *Santa Cruz (Calapor): profile of a village in Goa*, Panjim, Fernandes Publication, 1989.

ALMEIDA, José Julião do Sacramento, *A aldeia de Assolnã. Esboço histórico-arquiológico e biográfico*, editor Pe. João Cristovão Evaristo Almeida, Cidade de Goa, Tip. Singbal, 1958.

ANUÁRIO da Arquidiocese de Goa e Damão para 1955, coord. P. Francisco Xavier Gomes Catão, Bastorá, Tipografia Rangel, 1955.

AHMAD, Afzal, *Indo-Portuguese Diplomacy during the 16th and 17th centuries (1500–1663)*, New Delhi, Originals, 2008.

ARAÚJO, Francisco XAVIER de, *Capela de Nossa Senhora dos Milagres e de S. Tiago, Vanxém-Loutolim-Salsete. Goa. 1677–1947. Traços históricos*, Margão, Tip. Gomantak, 1947.

AZEVEDO, Carlos de, 'The churches of Goa', *Journal of the Society of Architectural Historians*, XV, 3(1956): 3–6.

———, 'A Arquitectura Religiosa', *Arte Cristã na Índia Portuguesa*, Lisboa, Junta de Investigações do Ultramar, 1959.

———, *A Arte de Goa, Damão e Diu*, Lisboa, Comissão Executiva do V Centenário do Nascimento de Vasco da Gama, 1969.

BOXER, Charles, 'The colour question in the Portuguese Empire, 1415–1825', *Proceedings of the British Academy*, XLVII(1961), 112–38, rep. *Opera Minora*, Fundação Oriente, Lisbon, 2002, III, 301–322.

———, *Race relations in the Portuguese colonial Empire, 1415-1825*, Oxford University Press, 1963.

———, 'The problem of the native clergy in the Portuguese and Spanish Empires', in J.S. Cummins, *The Missions of the Church and the propagation of the faith, Studies in the Church History*, Cambridge, Cambridge University Press, 1970.

BRAGANÇA PEREIRA, António Bernardo de, 'Os primieros cristãos e as igrejas de Salsete: 1558-1568 e 1570-1582', *Boletim Ecclesiastico da Arquidiocese de Goa*, 2, 4 (1946).

BRAGANÇA PEREIRA, António Bernardo de, 'Os primeiros cristãos e as igrejas das Ilhas de Goa', *Boletim Ecclesiastico da Arquidiocese de Goa*, 8,9,12,13 (1945).

CAETANO DO BEM, frei Tomás, *Memórias Historicas Chronologicas da Sagrada Religião dos Cónegos Regulares em Portugal e sua Conquistas na India oriental*, 2 vols., Lisbon, 1792–94.

CARITA, Hélder, *Palácios de Goa, modelos e tipologias de arquitectura civil Indo-portuguesa*, Lisboa, Quetzal, 1995.

CHICÓ, Mário Tavares, 'Aspects of religious art in Portuguese Índia - Architecture and woodwork', *Marg*, Bombay (1954): 13–25.

———, 'Igrejas de Goa', *Garcia de Orta*, special issue, Lisboa, 1956.

COSTA, Aleixo Manuel da, *Dicionário de Literatura Goesa*, 3 vols., Instituto Cultural de Macau-Fundação Oriente, Macau, 1998.

CRUZ, Caetano Otolini das Neves, *Memória histórica, descriptiva da aldeia de Cortalim...*, Nova Goa, Tip. Bragança & C[a], 1898.

DE JONGE, Krista, OTTENHEYM, Konrad (eds), *Unity and Discontinuity, architectural relationships between the Southern and Northern Low Countries (1530–1700)*, Turnhout, Brepols, 2007.

DIAS, Pedro, *O Espaço do Índico, História da Arte Portuguesa no Mundo*, Lisboa, Círculo de Leitores, 1999.

———, *Arte Indo-Portuguesa, capítulos da história*, Coimbra, Almedina, 2004.

———, *De Goa a Pangim, memórias tangíveis da capital do Estado Português da Índia*, Lisboa, Banco Santander Totta, 2005.

FARIA, Alice Santiago, 'Panjim between the past and modernity: building the city of New Goa, 1776–1921', *Murphy* 2 (2007): 66–97.

FERNANDES, Caetano da Cruz, 'Ancient historical documents regarding Saint John the Baptist's Church' in *Fourth Centenary. Saint John the Baptist's Church, Benaulim*, 1596–1996', 37–43 e 'Gleaning through history', idem, 47–53.

FERNANDES, José Manuel, 'Vestígios do Manuelino na arquitectura religiosa de influência portuguesa na Índia: Malabar, Coromandel, Goa', *Oceanos*, 19/20(1994): 136–154.

———, 'Urbanismo e Arquitectura no Estado da Índia (Índia Portuguesa): Alguns Temas e Exemplificações / A- o Urbanismo / B- a Arquitectura Religiosa', *Vasco da Gama e a Índia / Conferência Internacional / Paris, 11–13 Maio 1998*, Lisboa, Fundação Calouste Gulbenkian, 1999: 271–293.

FIGUEIREDO, Lúcia, *Velha Goa, guia arquitectónico*, graduation dissertation in architecture, typescript, Departamento de Arquitectura, Faculdade de Ciências e Tecnologia da Universidade de Coimbra, 2001.

FIGUEIREDO, Niceno de, *Pelo Clero de Goa: duas lendas: o Cisma de Goa e a Ignorância do Clero Goês*, Bastorá, Tipografia Rangel, 1939.

FONSECA, José Nicolau da, *An historical and archaeological sketch of the city of Goa*, Bombay, Thacker & Co., 1878. (rep. AES, New Delhi, 1986).

FRIAS, António João de, *Auréola dos Índios & nobiliarchia bracmana...*, Lisboa, Miguel Deslandes, 1702, 2[a] ed., Bombaim, 1892.

GOMES, Cipriano da Cunha, *Antiguidades pátrias: estudo histórico archeológico da Egreja de Nossa Senhora da Piedade na Ilha de Divar*, Bastorá, Tip Rangel, 1902.

GOMES, Paulo Varela, 'Les projets de Francesco Borromini et Guarino Guarini pour le Portugal', *Revue de l'Art,* Collége de France, Paris, no. 133/2001–3.

———, 'Ordem abreviada e molduras de faixas na arquitectura italiana, espanhola e portuguesa do Renascimento', *V Congresso Luso-Brasileiro de História da Arte,* Faro, Outubro de 2001, Universidade do Algarve, Faculdade de Ciências Humanas e Sociais, Faro, pub. Faro, 2002.

———, 'Portuguese settlements and trading centres', in Anna Jackson e Amin Jaffer (eds), *Encounters, the meeting of Asia and Europe, 1500–1800,*V&A Publications, Victoria & Albert Museum, London, 2004.

———, *Buçaco, o Deserto dos Carmelitas Descalços*, Coimbra, XM Editora, 2005.

———, 'Guarini e il Portogallo', *Guarini,* ed. Giuseppe Dardanello, Susan Klaiber, Henry A. Millon, Centro Internazionale di Studi di Architettura Andrea Palladio, Umberto Allemandi & C., Turin, 2006.

———, 'Bombay Portuguese - ser ou não ser português em Bombaim no século XIX', *Revista Portuguesa de História das Ideias*, n. 28(2007), pp. 567–608.

———, 'Three (and a few other) Bombay churches', *Mumbai Reader* n. 07(2007), pp. 244–253.

GONÇALVES, Sebastião, *Primeira Parte da Historia dos Religiosos da Companhia de Jesus, e do que fizeram com a divina graça na conversão dos infieis a nossa sancta fee catholica nos reynos e provincias da India Oriental*, pub. Coimbra, 1957.

GRACIAS, J.A. Ismael, 'Epitaphios na Igreja do Espírito Santo de Margão' in *Bibliotheca Pública de Nova Goa, Relatório do Anno Económico de 1892 a 1893*, Nova Goa, Imprensa Nacional, 1893, pp. 34–42.

HIBBARD, Howard, 'The early history of Sant'Andrea della Valle', *The Art Bulletin*, XLIII(1961), pp. 289–318.

HULL, Ernest R., Bombay *Mission History, with a special history of the Padroado question*, Bombay, Examiner Press, 1927.

KAMAT, Pratima, 'Mateus de Castro - a rebel', *Purabhilekh-Puratatva*, V, 2 (1987), 11–22.

KLAIBER, Susan, *Guarino Guarini's Theatine Architecture*, PhD dissertation, 2 vols, Columbia University, 1993.

KLOGUEN, Denis L. Cottineau de, *An historical sketch of Goa, the metropolis of the Portuguese settlements in India* (1831), AES, New Delhi, 1995.

KOWAL, David M., 'The evolution of ecclesiastical architecture in Portuguese Goa', *India and Portugal. Cultural Interactions*, ed. José Pereira and Pratapaditya Pal, Marg Publications, Mumbai, 2001, 70-87 (first published: *Mitteilungen der Carl Justi-Vereinigung*, 5(1993): 1–22).

KUBLER, George, *Portuguese plain style architecture, between spices and diamonds, 1521–1706,* Wesleyan University Press, Middletown, Connecticut, 1972.

LINSCHOTEN, Jan Huygen van, *Itinerário, Viagem ou Navegação de Jan Huygen van Linschoten para as Índias Orientais ou Portuguesas*, ed. Arie Pos and Rui Manuel Loureiro, Lisbon, CNCDP, 1997.

LOBO Sebastião José Lopes, *Igreja de Saligão*, Bastorá, Tip. Rangel, 1923.

LOPES, Maria de Jesus dos Mártires, *Goa Setecentista. Tradição e modernidade*, Lisboa, Universidade Católica Portuguesa, 1999.

LOURENÇO, José, *The parish churches of Goa, a study of façade architecture*, Margão, Amazing Goa Publications, 2005.

Mãe de Deus Church – Saligão, Goa 100 anos – Souvenir 1873/1973 (s.l., s.d.).

MASCARENHAS, Fr. Nascimento J., *A paen to an ophthalmologist, Prof Dr Gama Pinto*, Verna, New Age Printers, 2002.

———, *Mormugao's rich heritage*, Verna, New Age Printers, 2006.

———, *Follow me – Parish priests of the parishes of Bardez*, Corlim, Sahyadri, 2008.

———, *Follow me - Parish priests of the parishes of Ilhas*, Verna, New Age Printers, 2009.

MELO, C.M., *The recruitment and formation of the native clergy in India - 16th to 19th century*, Lisboa, Agência Geral do Ultramar, 1955.

Memória histórico-eclesiástica da Arquidiocese de Goa, 1533–1933, Nova Goa, Tip. A Voz de S. Francisco, 1933.

MENDES, António Lopes, *A Índia Portuguesa*, 2 vols. (1886), Lisboa, Fundação Oriente, 1992.

MENDIRATTA, Sidh, D. Losa, *A igreja e convento dos Agostinhos de Velha Goa, memórias de um levantamento*, graduation dissertation in architecture, typescript, Faculdade de Arquitectura da Universidade do Porto, 2003.

MITTERWALLNER, Gritli Von, *Chaul, eine Unerforschte Stadt an der Westküste Indiens*, Walter de Gruyter & Co., Berlin, 1964.

MOREIRA, Rafael, 'A primeira Comemoração: o Arco dos Vice-Reis' *Oceanos,* 19–20(1994), 156–159.

———, 'From Manueline to Renaissance in Portuguese India', *Mare Liberum* 9(1995), 401–407.

———, 'Goa em 1535, uma cidade manuelina', *Revista da Faculdade de Ciências Sociais e Humanas*, Universidade Nova de Lisboa, 8(1995), 177–221.

———, 'Riflessi della Ghiara nell'India portoghese: la chiesa dei Teatini a Goa', *La Basilica della Ghiara. Il miracolo della città*, Reggio Emilia, 1997.

NAZARÉ, Casimiro Cristovão de, *Mitras Lusitanas do Oriente...*, Lisboa, Sociedade de Geografia de Lisboa, 1897.

NORONHA, Alberto Eugénio Xavier de, *Galeria de Neurenses Ilustres: Monsenhor Francisco do Rego, licenciado e protonotário apostólico (1638–1689)*, Nova Goa: Tip. Bragança & Cia., 1919.

NORONHA, Percival de, 'Fontaínhas: vivendo com o passado', *Oriente*, 1(2001), 15–27.

OSSWALD, Maria Cristina, 'Goa and Jesuit cult and iconography defore 1622', *Archivium Historicum Societatis Jesu*, 2005: 155–181.

PAIS, Leonardo, *Promptuário das definições índicas...*, Lisboa, na Officina de António Pedroso Galram, 1713.

PEREIRA, António Nunes, *A Arquitectura Religiosa Cristã de Velha Goa. Segunda metade do século XVI - primeiras décadas do século XVII*, Lisboa, Fundação Oriente, 2005.

PEREIRA, José, *Baroque Goa*, Books & Books, New Delhi, 1995.

PEREIRA, José, 'The evolution of the Goan Hindu Temple', in José Pereira and Pratapaditya Pal (eds), *India and Portugal. Cultural Interactions*, Marg Publications, Mumbai, 2001: 89–97.

———, *Churches of Goa*, Oxford University Press, New Delhi, 2002.

PINTO, Rochelle, *Between Empires, print and politics in Goa*, New Delhi, Oxford University Press, 2007.

REGO, António da Silva, *O Padroado Português do Oriente e a sua historiografia (1838–1959)*, Lisboa, Academia Portuguesa de História, 1978.

RIVARA, J. H. da Cunha, *Inscripções de Diu, trasladas das próprias em Janeiro de 1859*, Nova Goa, Imprensa Nacional, 1856.

———, *Additamento às reflexões sobre o padroado portuguez no Oriente*, Nova Goa, Imprensa Nacional, 1858.

———, *Reflexões sobre o padroado portuguez no Oriente applicadas à proclamação pastoral do Rev. Fr. Angelico... / por um portuguez*, Nova Goa, Imprensa Nacional, 1858.

———, *O arcebispo de Goa e a Congregação de Propaganda Fide / por um português*, Nova-Goa, na Imprensa Nacional, 1862.

ROCHA, Leopoldo da, *As Confrarias de Goa: séculos XVI–XIX, conspectos histórico-jurídicos*, Lisboa, Centro de Estudos Históricos Ultramarinos, 1973.

———, 'Henrique Bravo de Morais e a sua 'Notícia Inédita': ensaio bio-bibliográfico', *Brotéria*, 109 (1979).

———, 'What the chronicler missed about Santa Monica of Goa: the untold story of a rebellion (1730–1734)', *Indian Church History Review*, 26, 2 (1992).

———, 'Uma página inédita do Real Mosteiro de Santa Mónica de Goa (1730–1734) e achegas para a história do padre nativo', *Mare Liberum*, 17(1999): 229–266.

ROSSA, Walter, *Cidades Indo-Portuguesas/Indo-Portuguese Cities*, Comissão Nacional para as Comemorações dos Descobrimentos Portugueses, Lisbon, 1997.

SALDANHA, Padre M.J. Gabiel de, *História de Goa, política e arqueológica*, 2 vols. Nova Goa, Livraria Coelho, 1925–26 (rep. AES, New Delhi, 1990).

Saligão, Golden Jubilee, 1936–1986, Bombay, 1986.

Saligão - Focus of a Picturesque Goan Village 1873/1973 (s.l., s.d.).

SEQUEIRA, P. Jorge Paulino, *Raia e Camorlim*, Pilar, Xaverian Press, 1972.

SERRÃO, Vitor, *Pintura e devoção em Goa no tempo dos Filipes. As encomendas agostinianas para o 'Monte Santo' (1602–1639)*, typescript report to Fundação Oriente, 2008.

SILVA, Tomás da, *Monumentos históricos e a casa paroquial de Cortalim*, Cidade de Goa, Tip. Araújo, 1951.

SOUSA, P. Francisco de, SJ, *Oriente Conquistado a Jesus Cristo pelos padres da Companhia de Jesus da Província de Goa*, Lisboa, na Officina de Valentim da Costa Deslandes, 1710 (rep. Porto, 1978).

SOUZA, Teotonio R. de, 'Moira: a peep into its past, some historical notes on Moira', *350 years Thanksgiving celebrations, Church of Moira, 1636–1986*, Alto Porvorim, 1986.

———, 'Colvale: bridging a tradition', *St. Francis of Assisi Church, Colvale, 4th centenary Souvenir*, 1991, pp. 6–10

TELES, Ricardo Micael, *Apontamentos para a história arqueológica dos Reis Magos*, sn., 1906.

TELES, Ricardo Micael, *Os franciscanos no Oriente e os seus conventos*, Nova Goa, Tip. Rau e Irmãos, 1922.

———, *Freguesia de Nerul: estudo histórico-arqueológico*, Nova Goa, Imprensa Oriental, 1925.

THOMAZ. Luís Filipe, *De Ceuta a Timor*, Lisboa, Difel, 1994.

TRINDADE, frei Paulo da, *Conquista Espiritual do Oriente*, 3 vols, ed. F. Félix Lopes OFM, Lisboa, Centro de Estudos Históricos Ultramarinos, 1962–1964.

VALLE, Pietro della, *The travels of Pietro della Valle in India*, 2 vols, Hakluyt Society, London, 1892.

CARTOGRAPHY

EREDIA, Manuel Godinho de, *Plantas das Praças das Conquistas de Portugal feitas por ordem de Ruy Lourenço de Tavora Vizorey da India, Por Manoel Godinho de Eredia Cosmographo em 610*, Original at the Secção de Estampas da Biblioteca do Rio de Janeiro, 3–1–33. Photographic copy at the Arquivo Histórico Militar, Lisboa: 3ª Divisão, 47ª Secção, n. 3730, AV2.

———, *Livro de Plantaformas das Fortalezas da India* (22 plans), Archive of the Forte de S. Julião da Barra.

RESENDE, António Barreto de (drawings), e BOCARRO, António (text), *Livro das Plantas de todas as Fortalezas Cidades e Povoações do Estado da India Oriental*, ca. 1632–1635. Original at Biblioteca Pública e Arquivo Distrital de Évora: CXV–2–1. Pub. BOCARRO, António, *O Livro das Plantas de todas as Fortalezas Cidades e Povoações do Estado da India Oriental*, 2 vols, Lisboa, Imprensa Nacional-Casa da Moeda, 1992. Second original at Bibliothéque Nationale de Paris, pub. in b&w *Arquivo Português Oriental*, 1936–40, Tomo IV, vol. 2. Several different versions: *O Livro das Plantas das Fortalezas Cidades e Povoações do Estado da India Oriental com demonstrações do maritimo dos Reinos e Provincias donde estão Cituadas e Outros Portos Principais daquelas partes*, Biblioteca do Paço de Vila Viçosa-Fundação Casa de Bragança, pub. Lisboa, Instituto de Investigação Científica e Tropical, 1991; CARNEIRO, António Mariz, *Descripçam da Fortaleza de Sofala e das mais da India com uma rellaçam das religiões todas que ha no mesmo Estado pello Cosmografo Mor Antonio de Mariz Carneiro, 1639*, original at Biblioteca Nacional de Lisboa: Cod Ilu. 149, pub. *Descrição da Fortaleza de Sofala e das mais da India*, Lisboa, Fundação Oriente, 1990. Another one at the Biblioteca Nacional de Madrid by João Teixeira Albernaz; at Sri Lanka's State Archives; the *Atlas* of 1663 at the Biblioteca da Ajuda, Lisboa, with drawings by João Nunes Tinoco; a copy of 1646 at the British Library.

SILVEIRA, Luís de, *Ensaios de Iconografia das Cidades Portuguesas do Ultramar*, 3 vols, Lisboa, Junta de Investigações do Ultramar, 1957.

Glossary

Academy/Academic culture: formal or informal associations of literati and cognoscenti typical of European high society circles of the 16th, 17th and 18th centuries.

Aisle: the same as a lateral nave; a passageway to either side of the central nave from which it is separated by colonnades or arcades.

Architrave: the part of the entablature resting on the columns' capital.

Articulate/articulation: verb/noun chosen nowadays to describe the manner or system in which is organized an architectural work.

Attic: low story or parapet sometimes placed above the cornice (in its usual sense, attic is the space found directly below the pitched roof of a house or other building).

Baluster and balustrade: baluster is a shaft in stone, wood or metal standing on a unifying footing and supporting the coping of a parapet or the handrail of a staircase, a veranda or a balcony. Multiple balusters form a balustrade.

Baptismal font/Baptistery: the baptismal font is a piece of church furnishing, normally carved in stone, used to perform the ceremony of baptism. Baptismal fonts can be located in spaces specially conceived for that function called baptisteries.

Baroque: according to traditional art historiography, baroque is one of the styles of Western architectural tradition. Given the immense variety of works of art called baroque, the term is nowadays applied to an epoch rather than a style: 17th and 18th centuries.

Barrel vault: semi-circular section vault.

Basilica/basilical plan or type: longitudinal church with a central nave higher than the lateral naves.

Bay: vertical parts or sections in which walls, internal or external, can be divided.

(Gian Lorenzo) Bernini: 1598–1680, important architect and sculptor who worked mostly in Rome.

Buttress: architectural structure built against, or projecting from a wall. Its purpose is to support or reinforce the wall.

Carolingian (dynasty or times): the term refers to the dynasty of Frankish kings who ruled north-western Europe between the 7th and the 10th centuries of the Christian Era.

Cartouche: a rectangular, square or oval decorative motive with an elaborate frame.

Carthusians: The Carthusian order, also called the Order of St. Bruno, is a Catholic religious order of enclosed friars.

Cathedral: in a Diocese, the more important church because it holds the seat (*cathedra*) of the bishop.

Catholic Reformation: used with the same meaning as Counter Reformation, it refers to the response of the 16th and 17th centuries' Roman Catholic church to the protestant Reformation.

Central plan churches: all churches in which, ideally, every main point is at the same distance from the centre. These churches can therefore be round, square, polygonal, etc.

Chancel: the same as main-chapel and similar to chevet. The part of the church in which the main altar is placed and from where mass is celebrated.

Chapel (main): the same as chancel.

Chapter: the body of clerics (canons and other church dignitaries) that advises the bishop, is in charge of the daily service of the cathedral and replaces the bishop in his absence.

Chevet: the same as main-chapel or chancel.

Choir: in a Portuguese or Spanish cathedral or church, the place or places from which the canons or priests participate in the mass. In some languages (English, French), choir also means the same as main-chapel.

Classical and Neoclassical: in the Western terminology of styles, classical refers to the culture of the Greeks and Romans and the Renaissance culture of the 15th and 16th centuries. Neoclassical is the revival of the Renaissance culture in the 18th and 19th centuries.

Clerestory: row of windows or other openings on the upper part of the church's side walls.

Cloister: enclosed patio in a convent or monastery.

Coffer: mouldings excavated on the surface of a dome or vault for aesthetical reasons and to diminish its weight. Coffers usually are square or polygonal.

Composite order: one of the architectural orders of the Western and Middle Eastern tradition. It was considered as the noblest of the orders because its main part (the capital) united the Ionic and the Corinthian capitals.

Corbel: also known as console or mensola, it is a piece of stone jutting out of a wall to carry weight or to appear as mere ornament below architectural elements such as window frames.

Corinthian order: one of the architectural orders of the Western and Middle Eastern tradition. Its capital is easily distinguishable by the motif of the acanthus leaves.

Cornice: the uppermost part of the entablature or the finishing moulding of a wall.

Counter-reformation: the same as Catholic Reformation.

Cross/crossing: the space in the church where the nave and the transept intersect each other.

Cupola: a small dome or the central part of a complete dome (which is composed of drum, cupola and lantern).

Deambulatory: in European medieval architecture, the gallery-like space that goes around the main-chapel of cathedrals or important pilgrimage churches.

Dome: a large cupola or the articulation of drum, cupola and lantern.

Doric order: one of the architectural orders of the Western and Middle Eastern tradition. It was considered the more austere and manly of the orders.

Early Modern Age: in Western historiography, the 16th and 17th centuries.

Elevation: the same as a façade but normally used when referring to interiors.

Entablature: the horizontal part of the order that rests upon the columns. It is divided into architrave, frieze and cornice.

***Ermida* (Plural: *ermidas*)**: very small countryside chapels.

(Filippo) Bruneleschi: 1377–1446, architect and sculptor from Florence, Italy.

(Francesco di GiorgioMartini): 1439–1502, architect and painter from central Italy.

Frieze: the middle part of the entablature. It can be decorated in different ways depending on the order.

Gable: the triangular portion of a wall between the edges of a sloping roof.

Galilee: the same as exo-narthex, a porch or portico placed against the church's façade.

Giacomo della Porta: c. 1533–1602, architect and sculptor who worked mostly in Rome.

Gothic/Neo-gothic: artistic and architectural styles, the first created in north-western Europe in the 12th century of the Christian Era, the second in several European countries in the late 18th or early 19th centuries.

Grotto: Italian word referring to an artificial cave created for recreational purposes in a palatial garden.

Hallenkirchen: or hall-church. German word normally used to describe churches where all naves have the same height and are supported by thin pillars or columns.

Lantern: uppermost part of a complete dome. It normally has the form of a little round columnar temple and it allows light into the building. But it can also be 'blind', that is, a simple shaft.

Late Medieval/Late Middle Ages: the late 14th and the 15th centuries in Western historiography.

Lateral chapel: chapels placed to each side of the main chapel or along the aisles or lateral naves.

Loggia: Italian word meaning a deep and wide veranda with columns or arches.

(Carlo) Maderno: 1556–1629, Italian architect who worked mostly in Rome.

Manueline: word used by Portuguese art historians to refer to the late-gothic art and architecture prevalent in the time of king Manuel I (r. 1495–1521).

Mensola (Plural: mensole): the same as corbel but with ornamental functions only.

Metopa (Plural: metope): one of the ornamental motives of the Doric order frieze.

Modern Age: the late 15th, the 16th, 17th and 18th centuries in Western historiography.

Monastic church: the church of a convent or monastery.

Mouldings (architectural): all ornamental architectural elements apart from those belonging to the orders: frames, pediments, friezes along the walls, cornices, coffers, etc.

Narthex: place immediately behind the entrance of a church and separated from its nave or naves by columns or pillars.

Nave: longitudinal parts of a church separated by arches, pillars or columns.

Oculus: round window.

Orders (architectural): an order is composed of the column and the entablature. The Middle Eastern and European architectural culture created five main orders from the ornamentally poorer and lower to the richer and higher: Tuscan, Doric, Ionic, Corinthian and Composite. Each order has different measurements and these determine the proportioning of the whole building (in theory at least).

(Andrea) Palladio: 1508–1580, Italian architect who worked mostly in the region of Venice.

Parti: French word referring to the architect's overall choice of the building's type and form.

Pediment: triangular moulding placed upon windows, doors or at the uppermost part of façades. Pediments can be closed, open, straight, undulating.

Pendentif: French-origin word referring to the elements that establishes the transition between a circular cupola and the square space that supports it.

Penetration vault: a barrel, planed, groin or rib vault the form of which is penetrated by the clerestory windows' projection.

Pilaster: a slightly projecting pillar applied to the face of a wall for ornamental reasons or to act as the embedding of the column of an order.

Pillar: supporting member with a square or rectangular section.

Pinnacle: element placed above the cornice of façades aligned with the columns or pilasters thereof. Pinnacles can also appear embedded in the façade wall. Their shape varies immensely, from the simple pyramid to the torch-like pinnacle.

Planed vault: a vault the section of which has the form of a basket handle.

Portaria/Porteria: Portuguese, Spanish and Italian terms referring to the door, room or rooms of a convent through which contact with the outside world could be established.

Priory: word used for the convents of many Christian orders or a religious building that has not reached conventual status yet.

Professed House: Jesuit building to lodge the trainees for priests who have already been admitted to the order.

Pseudo-solomonic: column with the whole of the shaft twisted or spiralled (the purely Solomonic column's shaft has non-spiralling parts).

Pulpit: elevated tribune in a church from where the priest's sermon or readings of sacred texts used to take place.

Renaissance: the cultural movement that took place in Europe from the late Middle Ages onwards with the objective of reviving the literature, the arts, the philosophy of Antiquity (in Mediterranean's culture terms, the millennium that ended in the 5th or 6th century of the Christian era).

Rib vault: vault or intersection of vaults supported by an armature of piped masonry.

Rocaille: ornamental fashion created in the 18th century in France and central Europe, which is characterized by a profusion of elements derived from the form of rocks, shells, plants.

Rustication, rusticated: ornamental treatment of pillars, corners or the lower parts of walls imitating stone surfaces.

Sacristy (or Vestry): part of a church where church vestments are kept and the priests prepare for mass.

Scrolls: the same as volute: the spiralling forms that connect higher to lower parts of a façade. The word can also be applied to any form that fulfils this role, even when it is not in the form of a spiral.

Sé: Portuguese word for Cathedral (from the latin *sedes*, the seat of the bishop).

Seminary: school for the training for priesthood.

Serlian (from Sebastiano Serlio): motives or compositions derived from the architectural treatise of the Italian Sebastiano Serlio (1475–1554).

Shaft: the cylindrical part of the column.

Solomonic: column with part of the shaft twisted or spiralled, believed to have been used in the Temple of King Solomon of Judea, the conception of which the Hebrew and Christian traditions attributed to God Himself.

Stalls: rows of chairs where the chapter's canons sat during mass.

Tabernacle: little templet where the Holy Sacrament is displayed in a church. The term can also refer to a pair of columns or pilasters supporting a pediment framing an altar or figure.

Talha: Portuguese word for the carving of wood for altars, pulpits, etc.

Tholos: Greek word referring to a little circular temple with columns all around.

Transept (inscribed transept; false transept): a longitudinal space inserted between the nave or naves and the chancel. If the transept does not protrude from the church sides it is called an inscribed transept; if it is only an arch located where the transept should have been, it is a false transept.

Treatise: architectural handbook or theory-oriented book written by Western architects between the 15th and the early 19th centuries.

Trent (and Tridentine): the Council of Trent (a city in northern Italy), bringing together Catholic cardinals and bishops and presided over by the pope, met for several sessions in the 1540s, 1550s and 1560s to redefine the orientation of the church after the protestant Reformation.

Type, typology: type (and the theory of type: typology) is the concept that allows us to highlight the architectural commonalities between buildings or parts of buildings that can be different from the formal point of view. For example, a rectangular single nave church is a type but these churches can vary considerably in dimensions, decoration, internal partitions, etc.

Under-choir: the part of the church below the choir situated upon the main entrance, common in Iberian churches. An under-choir is also an indo-narthex.

Vault (and vaulting system): a vault is an arch form over an empty space. It can be of stone, brick, wood. The vaulting system is the conjugation of the vaults with their supports and openings.

Groin Vault: the vault produced by the intersection at right angles of two barrel vaults. The groin is the edge of this intersection.

Volute: spiralling forms that connect higher to lower parts of a façade.

***Westwerk*/West front**: German and English words that describe the frontal part of churches sporting one or several towers and sometimes a transept. The type appeared in Carolingian architecture.